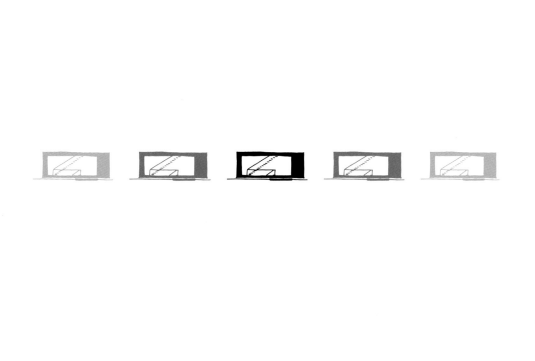

KÖNEMANN

© 2015 for this edition: koenemann.com GmbH

Distributed in cooperation with Frechmann Kolón GmbH

www.koenemann.com

www.frechmann.com

Published in the United States in 2016 by:

Skyhorse Publishing

307 West 36th Street, 11th Floor

New York, NY 10018, USA

T: +1 212 643 6816

info@skyhorsepublishing.com

www.skyhorsepublishing.com

Editorial project: LOFT Publications

Barcelona, Spain

Tel.: +34 932 688 088

Fax: +34 932 687 073

loft@loftpublications.com

www.loftpublications.com

Editorial coordinator: Simone K. Schleifer

Assistant to editorial coordination: Aitana Lleonart Triquell

Art director: Mireia Casanovas Soley

Design and layout coordination: Claudia Martínez Alonso

Editor: LOFT Publications

Introduction text: Aitana Lleonart Triquell

Layout: Ignasi Gracia Blanco

Translations: Cillero & de Motta, Mengès (FR)

ISBN 978-3-86407-322-9 (GB)

ISBN 978-3-86407-320-5 (D)

ISBN 978-3-86407-321-2 (E)

ISBN 978-1-5107-0454-1 (Skyhorse, USA)

Printed in Spain

There are several reasons behind the use of small homes. The most common are a limited budget and a shortage of land. In addition, when houses are used only occasionally and at certain seasons of the year, they do not have to be large in size.

Recent years have seen the development of new housing concepts and the reinvention of old processes and methods. An example are the compact, transportable modules that can quickly and easily be set up in different locations. This alternative way of life is similar to that of nomadic tribes, like the Bedouins, who still inhabit and roam the African deserts.

Prefabricated homes, yet another form of housing, are usually small in area. They have been carefully designed to the last millimetre and every single centimetre has been used in order to be able to provide all the necessary rooms and pleasant and comfortable living space.

This volume consists of four different chapters, which have been divided according to the area of each prefabricated home. The first, entitled TINY, looks at homes with a living area of no more than 270 sq ft. These are generally small extensions, bungalows, compact modules and tree houses. They show the extraordinary ingenuity of their architects, who managed to make the most of the space available. Open, multi-purpose spaces are a common feature of these tiny miracles.

The second chapter, entitled MINI, shows a selection of homes ranging in area from 270 to 538 sq ft. In this case, despite the fact that the area is still extremely small, the homes look more like conventional houses and the different areas are more defined.

Homes with areas of between 538 and 1,076 sq ft are dealt with in chapter three, entitled SMALL. In this case, the structure and layout of the spaces are more complete. This chapter also includes duplex-style apartments and even homes of several storeys, but where the total living area is still small.

To conclude, the chapter entitled COMPACT looks at houses with an area of just over 1,615 sq ft. These are, however, conventional homes where each room is an optimal space despite its size.

All of the homes in this book are a source of inspiration for people seeking to make the most of limited space, a small plot, or on a tight budget, but who do not want to give up on their dream home.

Die Gründe für die Projektierung von kleinen Wohnungen sind vielfältig. Die häufigsten sind das begrenzte Budget und die Raumknappheit. In anderen Fällen macht die zeitlich begrenzte Nutzung der Wohnung zu bestimmten Jahreszeiten eine großräumige Bebauung überflüssig.

In den letzten Jahren wurden neue Wohnkonzepte entwickelt, während gleichzeitig alte Verfahren und Methoden wiederbelebt wurden. Ein Beispiel dafür sind die kompakten, transportablen Module, die an verschiedenen Orten aufgestellt werden können und deren Installierung einfach und schnell ausgeführt werden kann. Diese alternative Lebensweise erinnert an Nomadenvölker wie die Beduinen, die in den afrikanischen Wüsten leben und diese Praktik noch heute ausüben.

Vorgefertigte Häuser, eine weitere beachtenswerte Alternative, haben normalerweise eine geringe Grundfläche. Sie sind auf den Millimeter genau entworfen, damit alle nötigen Zimmer darin Platz finden, wobei jeder verfügbare Zentimeter ausgenützt wird, um einen angenehmen und gemütlichen Raum zu schaffen.

Dieser Band enthält vier verschiedene Kapitel, die nach der Flächengröße der Wohnungen, die in jedem von ihnen gezeigt werden, aufgeteilt sind. Das erste mit dem Titel TINY beinhaltet die Entwürfe, deren Wohnfläche nicht über 25 m² hinausgeht. Es handelt sich im Allgemeinen um kleine Anbauten, Bungalows, kleine Module und Baumhäuser. Diese Räume zeigen den außerordentlichen Einfallsreichtum der Architekten, um die kleinsten Flächen so gut wie möglich auszunützen. Offene Vielzweckräume kommen in diesen kleinen Wunderwerken am häufigsten vor.

Das zweite Kapitel, MINI, zeigt eine Auswahl von Wohnungen, deren Grundfläche jeweils zwischen 25 und 50 m² groß ist. In diesem Fall weisen die Entwürfe, obwohl deren Fläche weiterhin äußerst gering ist, ein Erscheinungsbild, das sich den normalen Wohnungen annähert, bei denen die verschiedenen Bereiche mehr voneinander abgegrenzt sind.

Die Entwürfe von 50 bis 100 m² werden im dritten Kapitel mit dem Titel SMALL gezeigt. Diese Projekte weisen eine vollständigere Raum- und Organisationsstruktur auf. Dieses Kapitel enthält auch Apartments vom Typ Duplex (über zwei Stockwerke gehend) und sogar mehrstöckige Wohnungen, deren Gesamtwohnfläche aber weiterhin reduziert ist.

Zum Schluss enthält das COMPACT-Kapitel Wohnungen, deren Fläche kaum über 100 m² hinausgeht. Diese Entwürfe werden dennoch als normale Wohnung wahrgenommen, in jedem Zimmer trotz seiner Größe über eine optimale Raumaufteilung verfügt.

Jeder in diesem Buch aufgenommene Entwurf ist eine Inspirationsquelle für diejenigen, die das Beste aus einem kleinen Raum oder einem Grundstück von begrenzten Ausmaßen machen wollen, so wie für diejenigen, die über ein knappes Budget verfügen, aber nicht auf ihren Traum verzichten.

Les raisons qui se cachent derrière le succès des petits logements sont multiples. Les plus courantes sont la restriction du budget ou encore le manque d'espace. Parfois, lorsque le logement est destiné à un usage ponctuel et limité, pendant seulement certaines saisons de l'année, de grandes dimensions s'avèrent superflues.

Au cours des dernières années, de nouveaux concepts de logements ont été développés alors même que les procédés et méthodes traditionnels se voyaient réinventer. Un bon exemple de ce phénomène est l'apparition des modules compacts et transportables, qui peuvent être placés à différents endroits et dont l'installation est très simple et rapide. Ce mode de vie alternatif s'inspire des populations nomades, telles que les Bédouins, qui vivent dans les désert africains et conservent cette pratique encore aujourd'hui.

Les maisons préfabriquées, autre alternative à prendre en compte, ont généralement une superficie réduite. Leur conception est pensée au millimètre près afin de pouvoir contenir toutes les pièces nécessaires, en exploitant chaque centimètre disponible, et de créer un espace pratique et agréable.

Ce volume comporte quatre chapitres différents, répartis selon la surface présentée dans chacun d'entre eux. Le premier, intitulé TINY, regroupe les projets dont la surface habitable ne dépasse pas les 25 m². Il s'agit en général de petites constructions annexes, de bungalows, de petits modules ou encore de maisons dans les arbres. Ces espaces reflètent l'extraordinaire ingéniosité des architectes qui parviennent à tirer le maximum des superficies minimums. Les espaces ouverts et multifonctionnels sont les plus couramment utilisés pour ces petits miracles.

Le second chapitre, MINI, comporte une sélection de logements dont la superficie varie entre 25 et 50 m². Dans ces cas-là, bien que la surface reste extrêmement réduite, les projets ressemblent davantage à des logements normaux, avec différentes zones délimitées.

Les projets dont la superficie se situe entre 50 et 100 m² apparaissent dans le troisième chapitre, intitulé SMALL. Ces projets présentent une structure et une organisation des espaces beaucoup plus complètes. Cette section aborde également les appartements de type duplex et même les maisons à plusieurs étages, mais dont la surface habitable reste réduite.

Enfin, le chapitre COMPACT se concentre sur les logements dont la superficie dépasse à peine les 100 m². Toutefois, ces projets sont perçus comme des logements normaux, dans lesquels chaque pièce dispose d'un espace optimal malgré sa petite taille.

Chacun des projets décrits dans ce livre est une source d'inspiration pour toutes personnes cherchant à exploiter au maximum un petit espace ou un terrain aux dimensions réduites, ainsi que pour tous ceux qui disposent d'un budget limité mais ne veulent pas renoncer à leur rêve.

De achterliggende redenen voor het ontwerpen van kleine woningen zijn legio. Een beperkt budget en een klein perceel zijn de meest voorkomende. In andere gevallen hoeft de woning niet groot te zijn, omdat zij alleen in bepaalde periodes of slechts af en toe gebruikt wordt.

De afgelopen jaren hebben zich nieuwe woonconcepten ontwikkeld en zijn oude processen en methodes vernieuwd. Een voorbeeld zijn compacte en verplaatsbare modules, die naar verschillende locaties kunnen worden overgebracht en snel en eenvoudig te monteren zijn. Deze alternatieve levensvorm doet denken aan die van nomadenvolken zoals de Bedoeïenen, die tot op de dag van vandaag in de Afrikaanse woestijnen op die manier leven.

Geprefabriceerde huizen, een ander alternatief waar rekening mee moet worden gehouden, hebben gewoonlijk een klein woonoppervlak. Het ontwerp daarvan is op de millimeter nauwkeurig uitgedacht, zodat alle nodige vertrekken erin passen, waarbij iedere beschikbare centimeter maximaal wordt benut, om een aangename en comfortabele leefruimte te creëren.

Dit boek bestaat uit vier hoofdstukken die zijn ingedeeld afhankelijk van het oppervlak. In het eerste hoofdstuk, getiteld TINY, worden enkele projecten besproken waarvan het woonoppervlak niet groter is dan 25 m². Het betreft hoofdzakelijk kleine bijgebouwen, bungalows, kleine modules en boomhutten. Deze bouwwerken geven blijk van de buitengewoon knappe prestatie van de architecten om maximaal rendement te halen uit minimale oppervlaktes. Open en multifunctionele ruimtes zijn in deze kleine juweeltjes gebruikelijk.

Het tweede hoofdstuk, MINI, laat een selectie woningen zien van tussen de 25 en 50 m². In dit geval lijken de projecten, ondanks dat het oppervlak nog steeds erg beperkt is, meer op die van gebruikelijke woningen, waarin de verschillende vertrekken duidelijker zijn afgebakend.

Projecten van tussen de 50 en 100 m² komen in het derde hoofdstuk, genaamd SMALL, aan bod. Deze projecten hebben een completere structuur en indeling van de ruimtes. In dit onderdeel zijn ook appartementen van het type duplex en huizen met meerdere etages opgenomen, maar het totale woonoppervlak is nog steeds beperkt.

Het hoofdstuk COMPACT behandelt tenslotte woningen met een oppervlak van nauwelijks groter dan 100 m². Deze projecten worden echter beschouwd als normale woning, waarin ieder vertrek, ondanks zijn afmeting, optimaal wordt benut.

Elk van de projecten die in dit boek worden besproken vormt een bron van inspiratie voor degenen die maximaal profijt willen trekken uit een beperkte ruimte of een perceel met kleine afmetingen, en voor mensen die beschikken over een beperkt budget, maar toch niet willen afzien van hun droom.

I motivi che stanno dietro la progettazione di piccole abitazioni sono molteplici. I limiti di budget, ma anche lo spazio limitato sono i più comuni. In altri casi l'uso dell'abitazione circoscritto a determinate stagioni dell'anno rende innecessaria una costruzione di grandi dimensioni.

Negli ultimi anni sono stati sviluppati nuovi concetti di casa e sono stati reinventati i vecchi processi e metodi di realizzazione. Un esempio sono i moduli compatti e trasportabili, che possono essere sistemati in vari luoghi e la cui installazione è semplice e rapida. Questo modo di vivere alternativo ricorda quello dei popoli nomadi, come i beduini che abitano i deserti africani e continuano a seguire tale tradizione tutt'oggi.

Le case prefabbricate, un'altra alternativa da tenere in considerazione, hanno solitamente una superficie ridotta. La loro struttura è attentamente studiata al millimetro per ospitare tutti gli ambienti necessari sfruttando ogni spazio disponibile allo scopo di creare uno ambiente comodo e piacevole.

Questo volume si articola in quattro diversi capitoli, suddivisi in base alla superficie illustrata da ciascuno. Il primo, dal titolo TINY, raccoglie i progetti con area abitabile inferiore ai 25 m^2. Si tratta in generale di piccoli annessi, bungalow, mini-moduli e case sugli alberi. Questi spazi mostrano lo straordinario ingegno degli architetti per riuscire a trarre il massimo da superfici minime. Gli spazi aperti e multifunzionali sono ampiamente utilizzati in questi strabilianti progetti.

Il secondo capitolo, MINI, mostra un campione di abitazioni di dimensioni tra i 25 e i 50 m^2. In questo caso, nonostante abbiano una superficie estremamente ridotta, i progetti presentano caratteristiche più vicine a quelle delle case normali, con i vari ambienti maggiormente delimitati.

I progetti di dimensioni comprese tra 50 e 100 m^2 sono inseriti nel terzo capitolo dal titolo SMALL. Presentano una struttura e un'organizzazione degli spazi più completa. Di questa sezione fanno parte anche gli appartamenti a due o più piani, la cui area totale sia comunque ridotta.

Infine il capitolo COMPACT presenta abitazioni di superficie leggermente superiore ai 100 m^2. Questi progetti assomigliano molto a quelli di normali abitazioni, in cui ogni stanza dispone di uno spazio ottimale indipendentemente dalle sue dimensioni.

Ognuno dei progetti presentati in questo libro è fonte di ispirazione per chi desidera trarre il massimo da uno spazio ridotto o di scarse dimensioni o per chi dispone di un budget limitato ma non vuole rinunciare a realizzare il proprio sogno.

Los motivos que se esconden tras las proyección de pequeñas viviendas son múltiples. La limitación del presupuesto así como la escasez de terreno son los más habituales. En otras ocasiones el uso puntual y limitado de la vivienda a ciertas estaciones del año hace innecesaria una construcción de grandes dimensiones.

Durante estos últimos años se han desarrollado nuevos conceptos de vivienda, al tiempo que se han ido reinventando antiguos procesos y métodos. Un ejemplo son los módulos compactos y transportables, que pueden ser emplazados en distintos lugares y cuya instalación es rápida y sencilla. Esta forma de vida alternativa recuerda a los pueblos nómadas, como los beduínos que moran en los desiertos africanos y que mantienen esta práctica aún en la actualidad.

Las casas prefabricadas, otra de las alternativas a tener en cuenta, son habitualmente de superficie reducida. Su diseño está concienzudamente milimetrado para albergar todas las estancias necesarias aprovechando cada centímetro disponible y con el fin de crear un agradable y cómodo espacio.

Este volumen está organizado en cuatro capítulos en función de la superficie de las viviendas que aparecen en cada uno de ellos. El primero, titulado TINY, recoge aquellos proyectos cuya área habitable no supera los 25 m². Se trata por lo general de pequeños anexos, bungalós, módulos reducidos y casas en los árboles. Estos espacios muestran el extraordinario ingenio de los arquitectos para lograr sacar el máximo rendimiento a superficies mínimas. Los espacios abiertos y multifuncionales son los más comunes en estos pequeños milagros.

El segundo capítulo, MINI, muestra una selección viviendas cuya área oscila entre los 25 y los 50 m². En este caso, pese a que su superficie sigue siendo extremadamente reducida, los proyectos presentan una apariencia más cercana a las viviendas comunes, con las diferentes áreas más delimitadas.

Los proyectos de entre los 50 y 100 m² se recogen en el tercer capítulo titulado SMALL. Estos proyectos presentan una estructura y organización de los espacios más completa. En este apartado se incluyen también los apartamentos tipo dúplex e incluso casas de varios pisos, pero cuya área total habitable sigue siendo reducida.

Para finalizar, el capítulo COMPACT incluye viviendas cuya superficie supera escasamente los 100 m². Estos proyectos, no obstante, se perciben como una vivienda normal, en la que cada estancia dispone de un espacio óptimo pese a su tamaño.

Cada uno de los proyectos incluidos en este libro es una fuente de inspiración para quienes buscan sacar el máximo rendimiento a un espacio reducido o a un solar de escasas dimensiones, así como para aquellos que disponen de un presupuesto ajustado pero no quieren renunciar a su sueño.

12

TINY

JOSHUA TREE

Hangar Design Group // www.hangar.it // © Hangar Design Group

This mobile house, conceived as a holiday home in the mountains, recovers the spirit of the alpine refuges with its gabled roofs and beautiful views. The exterior cladding is made of steel, zinc, and titanium, laid in large sheets in the traditional way shingles are laid.

Dieses mobile Haus, das als Feriendomizil für eine bergige Region konzipiert wurde, lässt mit seinem Satteldach und den herrlichen Aussichten den Charme von Berghütten aufleben. Die Außenverkleidung besteht aus großformatigen Stahl, Zink- und Titanblechen, die wie traditionelle Holzpaneele angebracht wurden.

Cette maison mobile, conçue pour être une maison de vacances dans une région montagneuse, évoque les traditionnels refuges alpins avec une toiture à deux versants, offrant de jolies vues panoramiques. Le revêtement extérieur est composé de grandes lames en acier, en zinc et en titane et il est appliqué de la même façon que les bardeaux en bois traditionnels.

Deze mobilehome, ontworpen als vakantiewoning in een bergachtig gebied, straalt het karakter van berghutten met zadeldaken en prachtige vergezichten uit. De buitenbekleding bestaat uit staal, zink en titanium in grote platen die zijn aangebracht volgens de methode van traditionele houten dakpannen.

Questa abitazione mobile, concepita come casa per le vacanze in una zona di montagna, recupera lo spirito dei rifugi alpini con il tetto a doppio spiovente e la bella vista sul paesaggio circostante. Il rivestimento esterno è composto da acciaio, zinco e titanio applicato sotto forma di grandi lamine, utilizzando il metodo di posa delle tradizionali tegole di legno.

Esta casa móvil, concebida como residencia de vacaciones en una zona montañosa, recupera el espíritu de los refugios alpinos con sus tejados a dos aguas y hermosas panorámicas. El revestimiento exterior está compuesto de acero, zinc y titanio aplicado en grandes láminas mediante el método de colocación de las tradicionales tejas de madera.

Elevation

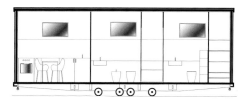

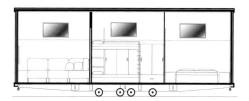

Sections

Floor plan

GIRAFFE TREE HOUSE

Andreas Wenning/Baumraum // www.baumraum.de // © Andreas Wenning

A maple in the lawn area was chosen to have the tree house built for a family of four. The design consists of a terrace suspended in the tree and a freestanding cabin built on nine slender steel posts. The result makes one think of a giraffe. The exterior is finished with Ipé boards and the interior is clad with jatobá veneer on plywood.

Un érable du jardin a été choisi pour recevoir la *tree house* de cette famille de quatre personnes. L'ensemble se compose d'une terrasse suspendue dans l'arbre et d'une cabane indépendante juchée sur neuf poteaux d'acier élancés. Le résultat fait penser à la silhouette d'une girafe, d'où le nom. La finition extérieure est en planches d'ipé ; l'intérieur est revêtu d'un placage de jatobá sur un support de contreplaqué.

Per costruire questa casa sull'albero destinata a una famiglia di quattro persone, gli architetti hanno scelto un acero in una prato. Il progetto prevede una terrazza sospesa sull'albero e una casetta indipendente poggiante su nove sottili pali d'acciaio. Il risultato ricorda la forma di una giraffa. L'esterno è decorato con listelli di Ipè e l'interno è ricoperto da fogli di jatoba su compensato.

Die vierköpfige Familie wählte einen Ahornbaum im Garten für die Errichtung ihres Baumhauses. Der Entwurf besteht aus einer am Baum hängenden Terrasse und einer freistehenden Kabine, die von neun schmalen Stahlpfosten getragen wird. Das Erscheinungsbild erinnert an eine Giraffe. Während die Außenfassade mit Ipeholz verkleidet wurde, wurde für den Innenraum mit Jatobaholz furniertes Sperrholz verwendet.

Voor dit boomhuis, bestemd voor een gezin van vier personen, werd een esdoorn uitgekozen. Het girafachtige ontwerp voorzag in een in de boom gehangen terras en een vrijstaande hut op negen slanke stalen palen. De buitenkant is afgewerkt met Ipé-planken en het interieur is bekleed met fineer van jatoba op gelaagd hout.

Para construir esta casa de árbol que sería habitada por una familia de cuatro miembros, los arquitectos eligieron un arce en una zona de césped. El diseño consiste en una terraza suspendida en el árbol y una cabaña independiente levantada sobre nueve delgados postes de acero. El resultado recuerda a una jirafa. El exterior está acabado con tablas ipé y el interior está revestido con chapas de jatoba sobre contrachapado.

ATELIER **FOR A CALLIGRAPHER**

Koshi Architect's Studio // www.kkas.net // © Koshi Architect's Studio

The building, leaning towards the view, was inspired by a ship's hull. At the same time, the parallelogram-shaped house acts as an awning over the entry. Inside, the experience is defined by the inclination of the walls and the openings which establish a relationship with the outside.

Das Gebäude, das sich zur Landschaft hin öffnet, wurde von einem Schiffsrumpf inspiriert. Der Baukörper in Form eines Parallelogramms dient als Vordach über dem Eingang. Im Inneren besticht das Haus durch die Neigung der Wände und die Fassadenöffnungen, die eine Verbindung nach außen herstellen.

La construction, ouverte sur un paysage, est inspirée d'une coque de bateau. La structure principale a également une forme de parallélogramme qui permet d'abriter l'entrée. L'intérieur se définit par des parois inclinées et des ouvertures qui le relient à l'extérieur.

Het gebouw, dat uitzicht op het landschap heeft, is geïnspireerd op de romp van een boot. Het parallellogramvormige hoofddeel fungeert als zonnescherm boven de ingang. Het interieur wordt bepaald door de inclinatie van de wanden en de openingen die het met de tuin in verbinding brengen.

L'edificio, inclinato verso il panorama, si ispira allo scafo di una nave. Allo stesso tempo, il parallelogramma della casa ripara l'entrata dal sole. L'interno è definito dall'inclinazione delle pareti e dalle aperture, che stabiliscono una relazione con l'esterno.

El edificio, que se abre hacia el paisaje, se inspira en el casco de un barco. Al mismo tiempo, el cuerpo en forma de paralelogramo sirve de toldo sobre la entrada. El interior está definido por la inclinación de las paredes y las aberturas que lo conectan con el exterior.

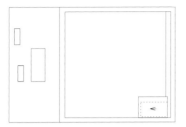

Roof plan

East elevation

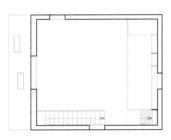

Second floor

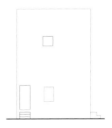

North elevation

Ground floor

Section

ZIG ZAG CABIN

Drew Heath // drewheath@ozemail.com.au // © Brett Boardman

The Zig Zag Cabin, a geometric dwelling that resembles a trailer without wheels. Inside the simple cubic structure of simple and well-proportioned lines, what can be seen appears to be controlled by the zig-zag shape that defines the window openings, creating views that are more closed or open depending on their configuration.

Die Zig Zag Cabin ist ein geometrisches Haus, das einem geschlossenen Anhänger ohne Räder ähnelt. Im Inneren der schlichten würfelförmigen Struktur mit gut proportionierter Linienführung bieten sich je nachdem, welche der zickzack-förmig angeordneten Fenster geöffnet oder geschlossen werden, unterschiedliche Aussichten.

La cabane Zig Zag est un logement géométrique qui ressemble à une caravane sans roues. L'intérieur de cette structure simple et cubique aux lignes bien proportionnées est défini par un motif en zigzag qui se remarque au niveau des fenêtres et qui crée des ouvertures plus ou moins larges, dépendant de leur configuration.

De Zig Zag Cabin is een geometrische woning die doet denken aan een oplegger zonder wielen. Binnenin de eenvoudige kubusvormige structuur met simpele en evenwichtige lijnen lijkt het uitzicht te worden beheerst door de zigzaggende vorm van de ramen, waardoor het zicht opener of geslotener is op grond van de opbouw.

La Zig Zag Cabin è un'abitazione che ricorda un caravan senza ruote. All'interno della semplice struttura cubica dalle linee pulite e ben proporzionate, la vista sull'esterno sembra essere controllata dalla forma a zig zag che definisce le aperture delle finestre, più o meno aperte in base alla loro configurazione.

La Zig Zag Cabin es una vivienda geométrica que recuerda a un tráiler sin ruedas. En el interior de la sencilla estructura cúbica de líneas simples y bien proporcionadas, las vistas parecen controladas por la forma zigzagueante que define las aberturas de las ventanas y crea vistas más abiertas o cerradas en función de su configuración.

WORLD OF LIVING TREE HOUSE

Young apprentices of Weberhaus in cooperation with other partners // © Alasdair Jardine

The tree house was built in the Weberhaus firm's World of Living Park to underline the innovative orientation of the company. It is fitted with glazing on all sides and is equipped with benches, drawers and small wooden tables on wheels. The interior of the curved walls and ceiling are covered with arboreal wallpaper.

Cette cabane perchée dans un arbre a été construite dans le World of Living Park de la société allemande WeberHaus, pour illustrer les tendances novatrices de cette entreprise. Elle est en bois vernis sur toutes ses faces, et dotée de bancs, de tiroirs et de petites tables en bois montées sur roues. L'intérieur des murs et du plafond courbes est revêtu de papier peint décoré d'arbres.

Questa casa sull'albero è stata costruita nel parco World of Living della ditta Weberhaus per esprimere la tendenza innovatrice dell'azienda. Possiede vetri su tutti i lati ed è equipaggiata di panchine, cassetti e piccoli tavoli di legno con rotelle. L'interno ricurvo delle pareti e del soffitto, è coperto di carta da parati con motivi arborei.

Dieses Baumhaus wurde im World of Living Park der Firma Weberhaus erbaut, um die Neuorientierung der Firma in Richtung innovativer Produkte zu unterstreichen. Es ist auf allen Seiten verglast und mit Bänken, Schubläden und kleinen Holztischen auf Rädern möbliert. Die Innenseiten der gewölbten Wände und der Decke sind mit einer Tapete mit Baummotiven ausgestattet.

Dit boomhuis werd gebouwd in het World of Living Park van Weberhaus om te laten zien hoe vernieuwend deze firma is. Het is rondom van glas voorzien en het meubilair bestaat uit banken, laden en houten tafeltjes op wieltjes. De gebogen wanden en het plafond zijn beplakt met behang waarop bomen zijn afgebeeld.

La casa de árbol se construyó en el Parque World of Living de Weberhaus para subrayar la voluntad innovadora de la empresa. Dispone de cristales en todos sus lados y está equipada con bancos, cajones y pequeñas mesas de madera con ruedas. El interior curvado de las paredes y el techo está cubierto de papel pintado con motivos arbóreos.

FINAL WOODEN HOUSE

Sou Fujimoto Architects // www.sou-fujimoto.net // © Iwan Baan

This small and original bungalow is made up of rectangular solid cedar blocks. Wooden pieces forming walls, ceilings, floor covering, furniture and windows have been arranged. In the interior, penetrating and protruding volumes become surfaces to sit down, take a nap, to climb or descend.

Dieser kleine, äußerst originelle Bungalow besteht aus rechteckigen Blöcken aus massivem Zedernholz, die Wände, Decken, Boden, Möbel und Fensterrahmen bilden. Im Inneren werden die Auskragungen zu Sitzflächen, Schlafgelegenheiten und Treppenstufen.

Ce bungalow, petit et original, est composé de blocs rectangulaires en bois de cèdre massif. Les pièces en bois formant les murs, les plafonds, le sol, les meubles et les fenêtres, ont été disposées. A l'intérieur, les saillies et les renfoncements se transforment en espaces servant à s'asseoir, s'allonger, monter et descendre.

Deze kleine, originele bungalow is samengesteld uit langwerpige blokken massief cederhout. De wanden, plafonds, vloer, meubels en ramen zijn met deze stukken hout gevormd. In het interieur veranderen uitstekende en inspringende delen in oppervlakken om op te zitten, te liggen, naar boven of beneden te lopen.

Questo bungalow piccolo e originale è composto da blocchi rettangolari di legno massiccio di cedro. I pezzi di legno sono stati disposti in modo da formare pareti, soffitti, pavimento, mobili e finestre. All'interno sporgenze e rientri diventano superfici in cui sedersi, dormire, salire e scendere.

Este pequeño y original bungaló está compuesto por bloques rectangulares de madera maciza de cedro. Las piezas de madera forman las paredes, los techos, el suelo, los muebles y las ventanas. En el interior los salientes y entrantes se convierten en superficies para sentarse, acostarse, subir y bajar.

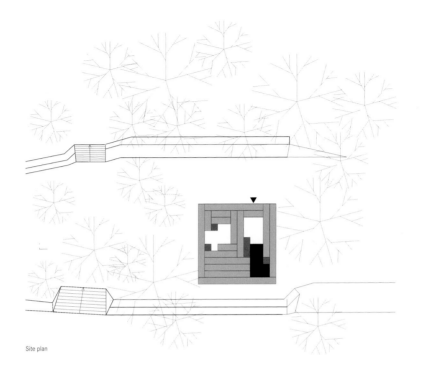

Site plan

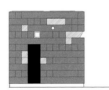   

Elevations

SUNSET CABIN

Taylor Smyth Architect // www.taylorsmyth.com // © Ben Rahn/A-Frame

Sunset Cabin sits on a wooden platform that extends past the cabin like a terrace and is used for the outdoor shower. Cedar paneling protects the shower from the sun, hiding both the shower and the interior of the house from sight since three of the four walls are made of glass.

La Sunset Cabin s'appuie sur une plateforme en bois qui est plus longue que la cabane et forme ainsi une terrasse qui constitue également le sol de la douche extérieure. Un revêtement en lames de cèdre protège cette douche du soleil, des regards indiscrets et de l'intérieur du logement, étant donné que trois des quatre façades sont en verre.

La Sunset Cabin poggia su una piattaforma di legno che si estende oltre la capanna come una terrazza, che è anche la base della doccia all'aperto. Un rivestimento a lastre di cedro protegge dal sole e dagli sguardi indiscreti la doccia e l'interno della casa, dato che tre delle quattro pareti sono in vetro.

Sunset Cabin steht auf einer hölzernen Plattform, die in eine Terrasse übergeht und außerdem den Boden für eine Freiluftdusche bildet. Da drei der vier Fassaden aus Glas bestehen, wurde eine Verkleidung aus Zedernholzpaneelen angebracht, welche die Dusche und das Innere des Hauses vor Sonnenlicht und fremden Blicken schützt.

Sunset Cabin staat op een houten platform dat zich verder uitstrekt dan het huisje zelf. Dit deel fungeert als terras dat eveneens de basis is voor een douche in de open lucht. De bekleding met cederhouten lamellen beschermt de douche en het interieur van de woning tegen de zon en tegen de blikken van buitenstaanders. Drie van de vier wanden zijn namelijk van glas.

Sunset Cabin descansa sobre una plataforma de madera que se extiende más allá de la cabaña a modo de terraza y que también es la base de la ducha al aire libre. Un revestimiento de lamas de cedro protege del sol y de las miradas ajenas la propia ducha y el interior de la vivienda, ya que tres de sus cuatro paredes son de cristal.

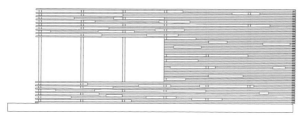

Elevation

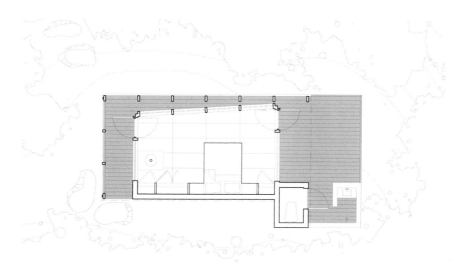

Floor plan

SCOUT TREE HOUSE

Andreas Wenning/Baumraum // www.baumraum.de // © Alasdair Jardine, Tim Mrzyglod

This two-level tree house is rented by a group of scouts during their stay at the campsite. The walls of the cabins are sided with larch boards both inside and out. The lower level is used as sleeping place for up to eight people. The living room, one meter higher is furnished with a mini kitchen and benches that can be turned into beds.

Cette « maison perchée » sur deux niveaux est louée par un groupe de scouts pendant leur séjour en camp. Les murs de la cabane sont revêtus de planches de bois, à l'intérieur comme à l'extérieur. L'étage inférieur sert de dortoir pouvant accueillir jusqu'à huit personnes. La « salle de séjour », un mètre plus haut, est dotée d'un coin cuisine et de bancs qui peuvent être transformés en lits.

Questa casa su un albero a due livelli è affittata da un gruppo di boy scout durante la loro permanenza nel campeggio. Le pareti delle due abitazioni sono rivestite da listelli di larice sia all'interno sia all'esterno. Il livello inferiore è utilizzato come spazio per dormire e può ospitare al massimo otto persone. L'altra sezione, più alta di un metro, è arredata con una cucina piccola e panche che possono diventare letti.

Dieses zweigeschossige Baumhaus wird von einer Pfadfindergruppe für ihren Aufenthalt auf dem Campingplatz gemietet. Das Untergeschoss dient als Schlafplatz für bis zu acht Personen. Das ein Meter höher gelegene Wohnzimmer ist mit einer Miniküche und Bänken ausgerüstet, die sich in Betten umwandeln lassen.

Dit boomhuis met twee verdiepingen wordt door een groep padvinders gehuurd. De wanden van de hutten zijn vanbinnen en vanbuiten bekleed met planken van lariks. De onderste cabine dient als slaapkamer voor maximaal acht personen. De wooncabine, die een meter hoger hangt, heeft een keukentje en zit-slaapbanken.

Esta casa en el árbol de dos niveles es alquilada por un grupo de exploradores durante su estancia en el campamento. Las paredes de las cabañas están revestidas con tablas de alerce tanto por dentro como por fuera. El nivel inferior se utiliza como espacio para dormir y en él caben hasta ocho personas. La sala de estar, un metro más alta, está amueblada con una cocina pequeña y bancos que pueden convertirse en camas.

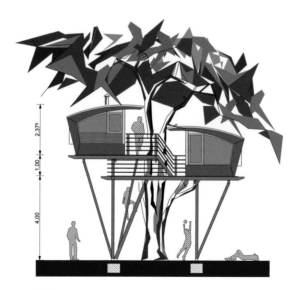

Elevation

BOX HOME

Sami Eggertsson Rintala // www.rintalaeggertsson.com // © Carlsen Are, Sami Rintala, Pia Ulin, Ivan Brodey

This 204 sq ft volume satisfies the basic needs of a home. Box Home, built by three people in four weeks, shows that a small house can be maintained and built using less resources, as this prototype costs a quarter of the price of a similar sized apartment in the same area of the city.

Dieser innerhalb von vier Wochen von drei Personen errichtete Baukörper mit einer Fläche von 19 m² erfüllt die grundlegenden Funktionen eines Zuhauses. Box Home beweist, dass ein kleines Haus auch mit wenig Ressourcen gebaut und instand gehalten werden kann, denn dieser Prototyp kostet gerade einmal ein Viertel eines Zuhause der gleichen Quadratmeterzahl im gleichen Stadtbezirk.

Cette construction de 19 m² comprend toutes les fonctions de base d'un logement. Box Home, érigée par trois personnes en quatre semaines, démontre qu'il est possible d'entretenir et de construire une maison avec peu de ressources ; ce prototype coûte en effet le quart du prix d'un appartement de la même surface dans le même quartier de la ville.

Dit blok van 19 m² voorziet in de basisbehoeften van een woning. Box Home, dat in vier weken door drie personen is opgebouwd, toont aan dat een klein huis met weinig middelen kan worden onderhouden en gebouwd. Dit prototype kost namelijk een vierde deel van een appartement met dezelfde vierkante meters in hetzelfde deel van de stad.

Questo volume di 19 m² soddisfa le necessità di base di un'abitazione. La Box Home, costruita da tre persone in quattro settimane, dimostra che una casa piccola può essere mantenuta e costruita con meno risorse; questo prototipo infatti costa un quarto di un appartamento con la stessa metratura, ubicato nella stessa zona della città.

Este volumen de 19 m² satisface las necesidades básicas de una residencia. Box Home, construida por tres personas en cuatro semanas, demuestra que una casa pequeña se puede erigir y mantener con menos recursos, pues este prototipo cuesta la cuarta parte de un apartamento con los mismos metros cuadrados ubicado en la misma zona de la ciudad.

Section

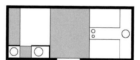

Ground floor

Second floor

CLIFF TREE HOUSE

Andreas Wenning/Baumraum // www.baumraum.de // © Andreas Wenning

This tree house is built on a rocky hillside near the Hudson River on the property of a family with children. The tree house, designed to match the style of the main house, is accessed via a bridge from the top of the cliff. The framework is sided with oak boards on the inside and with horizontal rough-sawn larch boards on the exterior.

Cette maison perchée est construite sur une pente rocheuse, près de l'Hudson, sur la propriété d'une famille avec enfants. Conçue pour s'harmoniser avec le style de la résidence principale, la Cliff Tree House est accessible par une passerelle depuis le sommet de la pente. L'ossature est habillée de planches de chêne à l'intérieur et de planches de mélèze brutes de sciage à l'extérieur.

Questa casa sull'albero si trova lungo un pendio roccioso nei pressi del fiume Hudson all'interno della proprietà di una famiglia con bambini. Alla casa sull'albero, progettata rispettando lo stile della casa principale, si accede mediante un ponte dalla sommità della collina. La struttura è ricoperta all'interno con tavole di quercia e, all'esterno, con listelli orizzontali di larice no trattato.

Dieses Baumhaus wurde auf einem felsigen Hang in der Nähe des Hudsonflusses auf dem Grundstück einer Familie mit Kindern errichtet. Das Baumhaus wurde im Stil des Haupthauses entworfen und kann über eine an der Spitze des Felsvorsprungs ansetzende Brücke begangen werden. Das Rahmengerüst ist innenseitig mit Eichenbrettern ausgebaut und außenseitig mit waagrecht verlaufenden, grob gesägten Lärchenholzlatten verkleidet.

Op een rotsige helling bij de rivier de Hudson is dit boomhuis gebouwd. Het ontwerp past bij de stijl van de woning. Vanaf de top van de klip geeft een brug toegang tot het boomhuis. Het geraamte is vanbinnen bekleed met eiken planken en vanbuiten met ruw gezaagde planken van lariks, die horizontaal zijn aangebracht.

Esta casa en el árbol se encuentra en una ladera rocosa cerca del Río Hudson dentro de la finca de una familia con niños. A esta cabaña, diseñada siguiendo el estilo de la residencia principal, se accede a través de un puente desde lo alto del risco. La estructura está revestida interiormente con tablas de roble y con tablas horizontales de alerce sin tratar en el exterior.

APULIA TREE HOUSE

Andreas Wenning/Baumraum // www.baumraum.de // © Andreas Wenning

This project was designed for a family with children for their property by the sea as a summer vacation stay. The tree house is partly suspended from the pines by means of steel cables and straps and partly resting on two flexibly mounted stabiliser supports. The solid wood frame is sided both inside and out with larch boards.

Cette réalisation a été conçue pour une famille avec enfants, dans leur propriété de vacances au bord de la mer. La cabane est partiellement suspendue aux pins au moyen de câbles d'acier et de sangles, partiellement montée souplement sur deux supports de stabilisation. L'ossature en bois est habillée de planches de mélèze, à l'intérieur comme à l'extérieur.

Una famiglia con figli ha voluto questo progetto per la sua proprietà di vacanze accanto al mare. La casa sull'albero è parzialmente appesa ai peni mediante cavi d'acciaio e poggia anche, in parte, su due supporti stabilizzatori fissati in maniera flessibile. La solida struttura di legno è ricoperta da tavole di larice sia all'interno sia all'esterno.

Dieses Projekt wurde für eine Familie mit Kindern als Ferienaufenthaltsort für ihr an das Meer grenzende Grundstück entworfen. Das Gewicht des Baumhauses hängt zwar zum Teil an den Pinien, an denen es mithilfe von Stahlkabeln und Riemen befestigt wurde. Zusätzlich wird es jedoch von zwei beliebig aufstellbaren stabilisierenden Stützen getragen.

Dit ontwerp werd gemaakt als zomerverblijf voor een gezin met een huis aan zee. Het boomhuis hangt met riemen en stalen kabels aan de dennen en rust op twee flexibel gemonteerde steunen. Het stevige houten skelet is zowel aan de buitenkant als aan de binnenkant afgewerkt met planken van larikshout.

Una familia con hijos encargó este proyecto para su finca de veraneo junto al mar. La casa del árbol cuelga parcialmente de los pinos por medio de cables y de correas de acero y se apoya también sobre dos soportes estabilizadores fijados flexiblemente. La sólida estructura de madera está revestida con tablas de alerce tanto por dentro como por fuera.

MICRO-COMPACT HOME

Horden Cherry Lee Architects // www.hcla.co.uk // © Sascha Kletzsch

M-ch draws on aeronautical and automobile design, while its scale and harmonies come from the architecture of the classic Japanese teahouse. Within its space of under 75-square-feet, this cube offers a space for each of the four basic requirements of a home: to rest, work, eat and wash.

M-ch s'est inspirée d'un design aéronautique et automobile. Ses dimensions et son harmonie rappellent l'architecture d'une maison de thé japonaise traditionnelle. D'une surface inférieure à 7 m², ce cube a les quatre fonctions de base d'un logement, offrant un espace pour se reposer, travailler, se nourrir et se laver.

La M-ch si ispira al mondo aeronautico e automobilistico; dimensioni e armonia si richiamano all'architettura della classica casa da tè giapponese. Questo cubo offre, in meno di 7 m², uno spazio per ognuna delle quattro funzioni basilari di un'abitazione: riposo, lavoro, alimentazione e igiene.

Das Design von M-ch wurde von den Bereichen Raumfahrt und Automobil inspiriert. Die Größenverhältnisse und die Harmonie gehen auf die Architektur eines klassischen japanischen Teehauses zurück. Auf seinen weniger als 7 m² Fläche bietet dieser Kubus Raum für die grundlegenden Funktionen eines Zuhauses: Schlafen, Arbeiten, Essen und Körperhygiene.

M-ch is geïnspireerd op het design van vliegtuigen en auto's en het formaat en de harmonie ervan zijn gebaseerd op de architectuur van een typisch Japans theehuis. In deze kubus van minder dan 7 m² wordt ruimte geboden aan elk van de vier basisfuncties van de woning: slapen, werken, eten en hygiëne.

La casa M-ch está inspirada en el diseño aeronáutico y automovilístico, y su escala y armonía beben de la arquitectura de la clásica casa de té japonesa. Este cubo ofrece, en sus menos de 7 m², un espacio para cada una de las cuatro funciones básicas de toda vivienda: descanso, trabajo, alimentación e higiene.

Longitudinal section

Floor plan

can touch

O₂

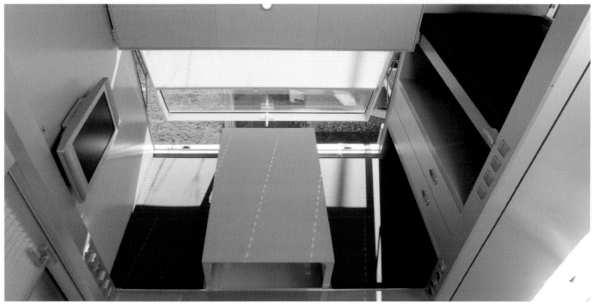

112

SMALL HOUSE **ON A HILLSIDE**

Vladimír Balda // www.balda.biz // © Ales Jungmann

The sloping grounds of the plot and its unfavorable orientation to the north were decisive factors that determined the shape of the house and its internal arrangement. Partly buried into the hillside, the house cuts into a massive retaining wall made of granite blocks of different size and shape.

L'inclinaison du terrain et son orientation défavorable au nord sont les facteurs décisifs qui ont influencé la forme de la maison et la disposition de ses espaces intérieurs. La maison, en partie enterrée dans la colline, interrompt un grand mur de soutènement composé de blocs de granit de différentes tailles et formes.

La pendenza e l'orientamento sfavorevole del terreno, rivolto a nord, sono stati fattori decisivi che hanno determinato la forma della casa e la sua disposizione interna. L'edificio, parzialmente interrato nel fianco della collina, penetra in un muro di sostegno massiccio composto da blocchi di granito di diverse forme e misure.

Die starke Neigung des Grundstücks und die ungünstige Ausrichtung nach Norden waren die entscheidenden Faktoren, die die Form des Hauses und die Gliederung der Innenräume bedingten. Das teilweise in den Hügel gebaute Zuhause liegt an einem großen Schutzwall aus Granitblöcken unterschiedlicher Größe und Form.

De hellende perceel en de ongunstige ligging op het noorden waren beslissende factoren die de vorm van het huis en de indeling ervan hebben bepaald. De woning, die zich gedeeltelijk onder de grond bevindt, onderbreekt een immense steunmuur met blokken graniet van verschillende grootte en vorm.

La inclinación de la parcela y su desfavorable orientación hacia el norte fueron factores decisivos que determinaron la forma de la casa y su distribución interna. La vivienda, que está parcialmente enterrada en la colina, interrumpe un muro de contención inmenso construido con bloques de granito de distinto tamaño y forma.

XXS HOUSE

Dekleva Gregorič Arhitekti // www.dekleva-gregoric.com // © Matevz Paternoster

Based on the existing dimensions, Dekleva Gregorič designed a summer house. The new building, which is north facing, is a rectangular house with an inclined roof in which several openings were made to allow the sun to illuminate the area indirectly during the day.

Ausgehend von den Abmessungen des bestehenden Baukörpers entwarfen das Studio Dekleva Gregorič dieses Ferienhaus mit rechteckigem Grundriss. In das Schrägdach wurden mehrere Öffnungen integriert, damit die Sonne direkt in die nach Norden ausgerichteten Wohnbereiche scheinen kann.

En partant des dimensions de la construction d'origine, Dekleva Gregorič ont conçu une maison de vacances. La nouvelle maison a une surface rectangulaire et une toiture inclinée comportant plusieurs ouvertures afin que le soleil illumine, de façon indirecte, la zone de jour orientée au nord.

Op basis van de afmetingen van het vooraf bestaande huis ontwierp Dekleva Gregorič een zomerhuis. De nieuwe constructie is een rechthoekige woning met een schuin dak waarin verschillende ramen zijn aangebracht zodat de op het noorden liggende dagzone indirect door de zon wordt verlicht.

Partendo dalle dimensioni del volume preesistente, gli architetti Dekleva e Gregorič hanno realizzato una casa estiva. La nuova costruzione è un'abitazione a pianta rettangolare con un tetto inclinato in cui sono state praticate varie aperture affinché il sole illuminasse indirettamente la zona giorno, orientata a nord.

Partiendo de las dimensiones del volumen preexistente, el estudio Dekleva Gregorič diseñó una casa de veraneo. La nueva construcción es una vivienda de planta rectangular con una cubierta inclinada en la que se practicaron varias oberturas para que el sol ilumine de forma indirecta la zona de día, orientada a norte.

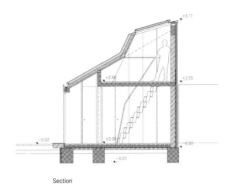

Section

Ground floor

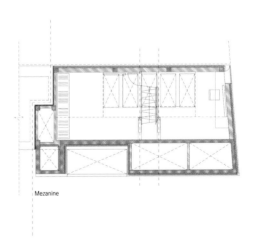

Mezanine

BOATHOUSE

Drew Heath // drewheath@ozemail.com.au // © Brett Boardman

One of the goals of this project was to redesign the concept of the boathouse. The project began with the installation of a covered railing on the deck around the boat that opens up the interior to the views of the ocean. This became a small pavilion that floats on the water.

L'un des objectifs de ce projet était de retravailler le concept de la maison bateau. Le projet a commencé avec l'installation d'un garde corps couvert sur le pont du bateau afin de créer un espace intérieur donnant sur la mer. Il s'est ainsi transformé en un petit pavillon flottant sur l'eau.

Uno degli obiettivi di questo progetto era riprogettare il concetto di una rimessa per le barche. Si è partiti dall'installazione di una griglia rivestita sulla copertura che circonda la barca, che consente di godere della vista sull'oceano dall'interno, per poi realizzare alla fine un piccolo padiglione galleggiante.

Dieses Projekt hatte zum Ziel, das Konzept des Hausbootes neu zu interpretieren. Zunächst installierte man an Deck rund um das Boot ein überdachtes Geländer. Die Innenräume öffnen sich zum Meer hin. Das Ergebnis ist ein kleiner Pavillon, der auf dem Wasser schwimmt.

Een van de doelstellingen van dit project was het concept van een woonboot te herontwerpen. Het begon met de installatie van een bedekte reling rondom het dek, waardoor men van binnenuit kan genieten van het uitzicht op de oceaan. Uiteindelijk werd het een klein paviljoen dat op het water drijft.

Uno de los objetivos de este proyecto era rediseñar un cobertizo para botes. El proyecto arrancó con la instalación de una reja forrada en la cubierta que rodea el bote, la cual permite disfrutar de vistas del océano desde el interior, y acabó por convertirse en un pequeño pabellón que flota sobre el agua.

iPAD

Andre Hodgskin Architects // www.architex.co.nz // © Andre Hodgskin Architects

The iPAD is a kitset designed to offer a wide range of possibilities. A single iPAD totals 540 square feet with just as much deck area. It can be grouped as a series of pavilions arranged in a variety of ways to form larger accommodation if required.

Le iPAD est un ensemble de modules conçus pour offrir une vaste gamme de possibilités. Un seul iPAD recouvre 50 m² avec un toit d'environ la même surface. Il peut s'assembler comme une série de pavillons qui peuvent se disposer de plusieurs façons pour former un plus grand logement si nécessaire.

iPAD è un kit di montaggio progettato per un'ampia gamma di soluzioni abitative. Un singolo iPAD è formato da un'area abitativa di 50 m² con una piattaforma esterna delle stesse dimensioni. Può essere montato come una serie di padiglioni che possono essere disposti in vario modo per formare, all'occorrenza, un'abitazione più grande.

Das iPAD House ist ein Ensemble aus mehreren Modulen, die vielfältige Möglichkeiten bieten. Ein einziges iPAD misst 50 m² und weist ein Schutzdach ungefähr gleicher Fläche auf. Die Module können als eine Reihe von Pavillons auf zahlreiche Arten angeordnet werden, um je nach Bedarf ein größeres Zuhause zu formen.

De iPAD bestaat uit een serie modules die zijn ontworpen om een keur van mogelijkheden te bieden. Eén iPAD neemt 50 m² in beslag met een overkapping van ongeveer dezelfde oppervlakte. De modules kunnen worden gegroepeerd als een reeks paviljoens die op allerlei manieren kunnen worden opgesteld om zo, indien nodig, een grotere woning te creëren.

El iPAD es un conjunto de módulos diseñados para ofrecer un amplio espectro de posibilidades. Un solo iPAD ocupa 50 m² con un cobertizo de aproximadamente la misma superficie. Los módulos pueden agruparse como una serie de pabellones dispuestos de múltiples maneras para formar una vivienda más grande, si es necesario.

Front elevation

Back elevation

Side elevation

Exploded axonometry

WEEHOUSE

Alchemy Architects // www.weehouse.com // © Alchemy Architects

Alchemy Architects successfully combines creative construction technologies with sustainable, modern designs. Without compromising the integrity of the basic module, limited to fourteen feet because of road restrictions, different combinations generate spaces of different sizes and layouts.

Alchemy Architects allie, avec succès, des techniques de construction créatives et des designs modernes et durables. Il existe toute une série de combinaisons qui créent des espaces aux dimensions et à la disposition variées, tout en préservant l'intégrité du module de base, réduit à 4,3 m en raison des limitations imposées par cette rue.

Alchemy coniuga con successo tecnologie creative per l'edilizia e progetti sostenibili e moderni. Senza compromettere l'integrità del modulo di base (circa 4,3 m per rispettare le limitazioni stradali), combinazioni diverse danno vita a spazi di varie forme e dimensioni.

Alchemy Architects verbindet kreative Bautechniken erfolgreich mit modernen und nachhaltigen Designs. Ohne die Vollständigkeit des Basismoduls einzuschränken, das aufgrund der bestehenden Straßenverhältnisse auf eine Größe von 4,3 m begrenzt wurde, gibt es eine Vielzahl von Kombinationsmöglichkeiten, die Räume in unterschiedlicher Größe und Anordnung entstehen lassen.

Alchemy Architects combineert succesvol creatieve bouwtechnologieën met moderne en duurzame ontwerpen. Zonder afbreuk te doen aan de integriteit van de basismodule, die slechts 4,3 groot is vanwege de door de straat opgelegde beperkingen, zijn er allerlei combinaties mogelijk die ruimten van verschillende grootte en indeling doen ontstaan.

Alchemy Architects combina con éxito las tecnologías de la construcción de corte creativo con diseños modernos y sostenibles. Sin menoscabar la integridad del módulo básico, que se reduce a 4,3 m debido a las limitaciones que imponía la calle, hay toda una serie de combinaciones que generan espacios de distintas dimensiones y disposición.

YOGA STUDIO / GUEST HOUSE

Carter + Burton Architecture // www.carterburton.com // © Daniel Afzal

The limited size of an existing house created the necessity for more space for friends and family and the privacy needed to meditate and enjoy yoga in a natural setting. The studio allows for some independence while staying connected enough to the main house for shared functions.

En raison des dimensions limitées de la maison déjà construite, l'espace utilisé par la famille et les amis ou pour méditer et pratiquer le yoga de manière plus intime dans un cadre naturel, a été agrandi. Le studio offre plus d'indépendance tout en restant près de la maison principale, avec laquelle il partage quelques fonctions.

Dalle dimensioni limitate di una casa esistente è sorta l'esigenza di disporre di più spazio per gli amici e la famiglia, oltre che della privacy necessaria per meditare e fare yoga in un ambiente naturale. L'edificio consente una certa indipendenza pur restando a breve distanza dalla casa principale per usufruire delle funzioni condivise.

Aufgrund der begrenzten Abmessungen des bestehenden Hauses entstand die Notwendigkeit, über mehr Platz für Freunde und Familie zu verfügen sowie für ungestörte Meditation und Yoga inmitten der natürlichen Umgebung. Das Studio wirkt unabhängig, befindet sich jedoch ganz in der Nähe des Haupthauses, mit dem es einige Funktionen teilt.

Door de beperkte afmetingen van het reeds bestaande huis hadden de eigenaars de behoefte om over meer ruimte voor vrienden en familie te beschikken en om in een natuurlijke omgeving te kunnen mediteren en op intieme wijze yoga te kunnen beoefenen. De studio geeft een gevoel van onafhankelijkheid, maar staat in de buurt van het hoofdhuis en deelt daar enkele functies mee.

Las limitadas dimensiones de una casa ya existente crearon la necesidad de disponer de más espacio para los amigos y la familia, y para poder meditar y practicar el yoga de manera íntima en un entorno natural. El estudio ofrece sensación de independencia, pero no deja de estar cerca de la casa principal y comparte con ella algunas funciones.

SUMMER CONTAINER

Markku Hedman // markku.hedman@hut.fi // © Markku Hedman

This portable prototype container has a rectangular structure constructed completely from wood that can be used as a refuge and a vacation home. It functions on the principle of a matchbox: a closed, hermetic cube while being transported, once installed the shutters over the window and the door can be opened to expand the house outwards.

Ce prototype de conteneur portable a une structure rectangulaire entièrement faite en bois et peut servir de refuge ou de maison de vacances. Il fonctionne comme une boîte d'allumettes : un cube, fermé et hermétique lorsqu'il est transporté et qui s'ouvre vers l'extérieur avec l'installation de volets autour des fenêtres et d'une porte.

Questo prototipo di container portatile presenta una struttura rettangolare realizzata totalmente in legno. Può essere utilizzato come rifugio o come casa per le vacanze. Funziona applicando il principio di una scatola di fiammiferi: durante il trasporto è un cubo ermetico chiuso mentre, una volta installato, le controfinestre e le porte si aprono allargando la casa verso l'esterno.

Dieser mobile Container-Prototyp mit rechteckigem Grundriss, der vollständig aus Holz gefertigt wurde, kann als Rückzugsort und Ferienhaus genutzt werden. Der Bau funktioniert nach dem Prinzip einer Streichholzschachtel: beim Transport handelt es sich um einen hermetisch verschlossenen Würfel, nach dem Aufstellen können die Blenden über Fenster und Tür geöffnet werden, um das Haus mit dem Außenbereich zu verbinden.

Dit prototype draagbare container heeft een volledig uit hout vervaardigde rechthoekige draagconstructie. Het kan gebruikt worden als berghut of als vakantiewoning. Het fungeert als een doosje lucifers: tijdens het transport is het een hermetisch afgesloten kubus en eenmaal geïnstalleerd en met geopende vensterluiken en deuren, wordt het een naar buiten toe gericht huis.

Este prototipo de contenedor portátil presenta una estructura rectangular fabricada íntegramente en madera. Puede utilizarse a modo de refugio o como casa de vacaciones. Funciona de acuerdo con el principio de una caja de cerillas: durante el transporte es un cubo hermético y cerrado y, una vez instalado, las contraventanas y las puertas se abren y amplían la casa hacia el exterior.

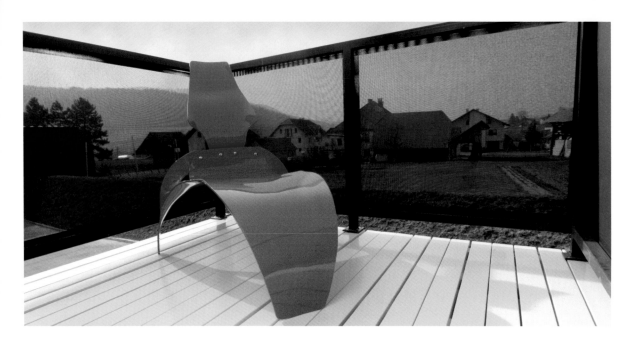

CONHOUSE 2+

Jure Kotnik // www.jurekotnik.com // © ConHouse

ConHouse is a housing systems consisting of containers that have been fitted out to offer the same quality of life as traditional homes. This has been possible thanks to an intelligent distribution of space, carefully selected materials and well-lit interiors.

Das Wohnsystem ConHouse besteht aus umgestalteten Containern, die die gleiche Lebensqualität bieten wie herkömmliche Häuser. Möglich ist dies dank der intelligenten Raumaufteilung, der sorgfältigen Auswahl der Materialien und der gut ausgeleuchteten Zimmer.

ConHouse est un ensemble d'habitations constitué de conteneurs qui ont été aménagés afin d'offrir la même qualité de vie que les maisons traditionnelles. Ceci a été rendu possible grâce à une distribution judicieuse de l'espace, une sélection soigneuse des matériaux et des intérieurs bien éclairés.

ConHouse is een woonsysteem bestaand uit containers die zijn aangepast om dezelfde levenskwaliteit te bieden als traditionele huizen. Dit is mogelijk dankzij een intelligente verdeling van de ruimte, zorgvuldig uitgekozen materialen en goed verlichte interieurs.

ConHouse è un sistema abitativo composto da container adattati per offrire la stessa qualità di vita delle case tradizionali. Tutto questo è stato possibile grazie a una distribuzione intelligente dello spazio, un'attenta selezione dei materiali e interni ben illuminati.

ConHouse es un sistema habitacional compuesto por contenedores que han sido acondicionados para ofrecer la misma calidad de vida que las casas tradicionales. Esto ha sido posible gracias a una distribución inteligente del espacio, una cuidadosa selección de los materiales y unos interiores bien iluminados.

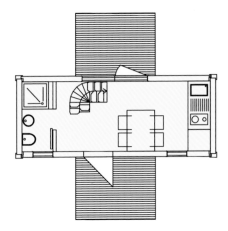

Ground floor

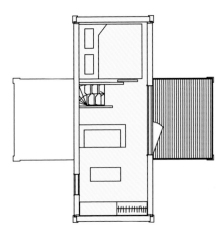

Second floor

PALUDO APARTMENT

Leo de Carlo, Roberta Angelini // www.leodecarlo.com // © Oliver Hass

The apartment occupies a section of a pre-existing industrial building. The whole interior was refinished in oak paneling. This was a common practice between the fifteenth and seventeenth centuries when naval workers from the Arsenale (naval yard) were hired to finish the interiors of administrative offices.

L'appartement se situe dans un ancien bâtiment industriel. Toutes les parois intérieures sont recouvertes de panneaux en bois de chêne, une technique répandue entre le XVe et le XVIIe siècle, lorsque les travailleurs de l'Arsenal (le chantier naval) étaient employés pour terminer les intérieurs des bureaux administratifs.

L'appartamento occupa una porzione di un edificio industriale preesistente. Tutto l'interno è stato rifinito con pannelli in quercia: questa era una pratica comune tra il XV e il XVII secolo, quando s'impiegava i marittimi dell'Arsenale per far rifinire gli interni degli uffici amministrativi.

Diese Wohnung belegt einen Teil eines ehemaligen Industriegebäudes. Die gesamten Innenräume waren – wie es vom 15. bis zum 17. Jahrhundert üblich war – mit Eichenholzpaneelen verkleidet. Damals hatte man die Arbeiter des Arsenals (der Schiffswerft) herangezogen, um die Bauarbeiten in den Verwaltungs- und Büroräumen zu beenden.

Het appartement neemt een deel van een oud fabrieksgebouw in beslag. Het hele interieur was bekleed met eiken planken, wat tussen de vijftiende en zeventiende eeuw, toen de scheepswerkers van de Arsenale (de scheepswerven) in dienst werden genomen om het interieur van de kantoren af te ronden, een gebruikelijke praktijk was.

El apartamento ocupa una parte de un antiguo edificio industrial. Todo el interior estaba revestido de paneles de roble, una práctica común entre los siglos XV y XVII, cuando los trabajadores navales del Arsenale (los astilleros) fueron empleados para terminar los interiores de las oficinas administrativas.

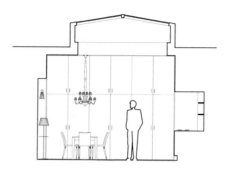

Section

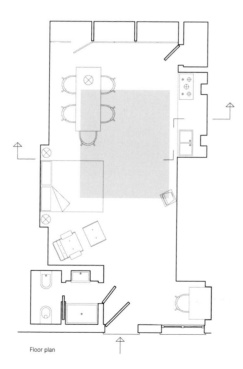

Floor plan

LAYER HOUSE

Hiroaki Ohtani // www.nikken.co.jp // © Kouji Okamoto

The goal of the architect was to create the richest and mots spacious interior possible. The structure is built like a trellis made of horizontal wood boards that alternate with empty spaces between them. The result is a room measuring 9 feet 4 inches wide by 25 feet deep.

Das Ziel des Architekten bestand darin, ein möglichst vielfältiges und geräumiges Interieur zu schaffen. Die äußere Struktur wurde wie ein Spalier aus waagerechten Holzbrettern gestaltet, die sich mit leeren Zwischenräumen abwechseln. Das Ergebnis ist ein 2,9 m breiter und 7,6 m langer Raum.

L'objectif de l'architecte était de concevoir l'espace intérieur le plus spacieux et le plus luxueux possible. La structure a l'aspect d'un treillis, composée de panneaux en bois horizontaux régulièrement espacés. Le résultat est une pièce de 2,9 mètres de largeur et de 7,6 mètres de longueur.

De bedoeling van de architect was een zo groot en gunstig mogelijke ruimte te creëren. De draagconstructie bestaat uit een soort rasterwerk met horizontale houten panelen en lege ruimten ertussen. Het resultaat is een vertrek van 2,9 m breed en 7,6 m diep.

L'obiettivo dell'architetto era quello di creare un ambiente interno che fosse il più spazioso e funzionale possibile. La struttura è costruita come una griglia composta da lastre di legno orizzontali intercalate da spazi vuoti. Il risultato è una stanza di 2,9 m di larghezza per 7,6 m di profondità.

El propósito del arquitecto era crear el interior más espacioso y óptimo posible. La estructura está construida a modo de enrejado compuesto de placas de madera horizontales intercaladas con espacios vacíos. El resultado es una estancia de 2,9 m de anchura por 7,6 m de profundidad.

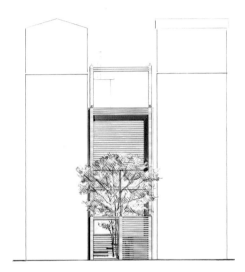

Elevation

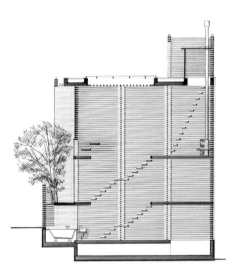

Section

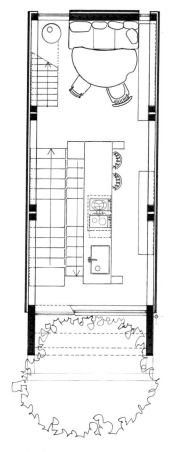

Floor plan

MONOLOCALE

Andrea Lupacchini // architer@libero.it // © Beatrice Pediconi

In this small space, just 301-square-feet by 10-feet tall, all of the functions of a regular one-bedroom apartment have been inserted like interlocking puzzle pieces. Each functional space has been given a volumetric area to occupy that has been sculpted into the most efficient form.

Diese Wohnung hat eine Fläche von 28 m² und ist 3 m hoch. Hier wurden sämtliche Funktionen eines herkömmlichen Ein-Zimmer-Apartments wie Puzzleteile miteinander verbunden. Allen Bereichen wurde ein bestimmtes Raumvolumen zugeteilt, das auf effektive Weise gestaltet wurde.

Cet espace a une surface de 28 m² et une hauteur de 3 mètres. Telles les pièces d'un puzzle, toutes les fonctions d'un appartement conventionnel avec une chambre sont intégrées à une même pièce. Tous les espaces fonctionnels sont dotés d'une surface volumétrique qui a été sculptée de la manière la plus efficace possible.

Deze ruimte heeft een oppervlakte van 28 m² en is 3 m hoog. Alle functies van een traditionele flat werden erin opgenomen alsof het om in elkaar passende puzzelstukjes gaat. Alle functionele vertrekken hebben een bepaalde ruimte toegewezen, waaraan op efficiënte wijze vorm is gegeven.

In questo spazio minuscolo di soli 28 m², con un'altezza di 3 m, sono state inserite come in un puzzle tutte le funzioni di un normale appartamento con una camera da letto. A ciascuna funzione è stata dedicata una determinata volumetria scolpita scegliendo la forma più efficace.

Este espacio tiene una superficie de 28 m² y 3 m de altura. En él se insertaron todas las funciones de un apartamento convencional de un dormitorio como si fueran las piezas de un puzzle entrelazadas. Todos los espacios funcionales tienen asignados una superficie volumétrica que se ha esculpido de la forma más eficiente.

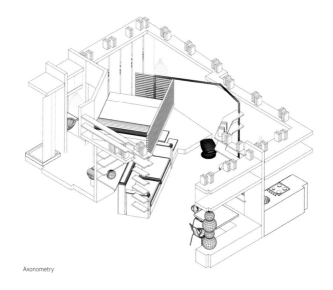

Axonometry

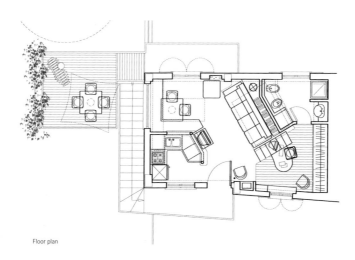

Floor plan

LODGE HOUSE

Guerrilla Office Architects // www.g-o-a.be // © Goa

An existing out-building in the backyard or a row house (student housing in a previous life) was stripped of its stone façade and converted to a guest cottage. In place of the stone facing is a two-story glass wall opening onto the garden.

Einige bestehende Räumlichkeiten im Hinterhof und ein Reihenhaus (früher ein Zuhause für Studenten) wurden ihrer Steinfassade beraubt und in ein kleines ländliches Gästehaus verwandelt. Anstelle der Fassade wurde zum Garten hin über zwei Etagen eine Glaswand installiert.

Quelques dépendances qui existaient déjà dans le patio arrière, ou provenant d'une ancienne maison adossée qui était autrefois un logement étudiant, ont été transformées en une petite maison de campagne pour les invités. L'ancienne façade en pierre a été remplacée par une paroi vitrée qui s'étend sur les deux étages et donne vue sur le jardin.

Een aantal reeds bestaande bijgebouwen op de achterpatio of een geschakelde woning (voormalig studentenhuis) werden van hun stenen gevel ontnomen en omgebouwd tot een buitenhuis voor logees. In plaats van de gevel werd een twee verdiepingen hoge glaswand die op de tuin uitkomt geïnstalleerd.

Un edificio esterno nel cortile posteriore o una casa a schiera (che ospitava studenti in una vita precedente): eliminata la facciata in pietra, ora è un cottage per gli ospiti. Al posto del rivestimento in pietra della facciata, una parete in vetro a due piani apre la casa al giardino.

Unas dependencias ya existentes en el patio trasero o una casa adosada (vivienda de estudiantes en una vida anterior) se desproveyeron de su fachada de piedra y se convirtieron en una casita de campo para invitados. En lugar de la fachada se dispuso una pared acristalada de dos plantas que da a un jardín.

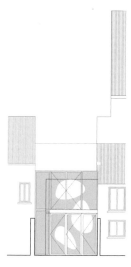

Back elevation

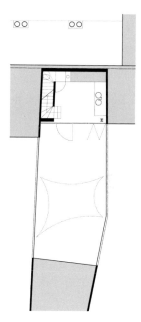

Ground floor

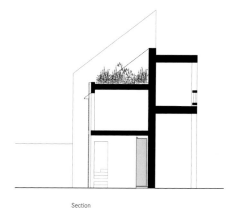

Section

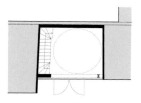

Second floor

MINI HOME

Altius Architecture Inc. & Sustain Design Studio // andy@sustain.ca // © Altius Architecture Inc. & Sustain Design Studio

The Mini Home is a self-contained, sustainable and modular response to environmental issues, and the increasingly high prices of real estate and resources. The construction materials were carefully selected for their durability and minor environmental impact without sacrificing the visual aspect.

Mini Home ist die kompakte, nachhaltige und modulare Antwort auf die wachsenden Umweltprobleme und die immer weiter steigenden Preise von Immobilien und Ressourcen. Die Baumaterialien wurde sorgfältig ausgewählt: Sie sollten langlebig sein, minimale Umweltwirkungen verursachen und die Ästhetik nicht beeinträchtigen.

Mini Home offre une solution compacte, durable et modulaire aux problèmes environnementaux et au prix (de plus en plus élevé) des immeubles et des ressources. Les matériaux de construction ont été choisis avec attention afin d'être durables et d'avoir un impact environnemental minime, sans pour autant affecter l'aspect visuel de la maison.

Mini Home is de compacte, duurzame en modulaire oplossing voor de milieuproblemen en steeds hogere prijzen van het vastgoed en de hulpbronnen. De bouwmaterialen werden zorgvuldig uitgekozen omdat ze duurzaam waren en een minimale impact op het milieu hebben zonder dat ze er minder mooi uitzien.

Questa casa è una risposta autosufficiente, sostenibile e modulare ai problemi ambientali e al continuo aumento dei prezzi delle proprietà immobiliari e delle risorse. I materiali da costruzione sono stati selezionati con cura per la loro durevolezza e il minore impatto ambientale, senza sacrificare l'aspetto estetico.

Mini Home es la respuesta compacta, sostenible y modular a los problemas medioambientales y al precio, cada vez más elevado, de los inmuebles y los recursos. Los materiales de construcción se seleccionaron cuidadosamente por ser duraderos y tener un impacto medioambiental mínimo sin sacrificar el aspecto visual.

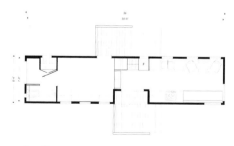

Ground floor

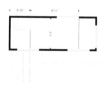

Second floor

FLAT

Matali Crasset/Matali Crasset Productions, in collaboration with Marco Salgado and Francis Fichot // www.matalicrasset.com // © Patrick Gries

The French designer Matali Crasset designed this home in the centre of Paris. Measuring 600 square feet, the home is laid out on one level and the rooms are distributed around the kitchen which opens out onto the dining area and living room without the use of any doors.

Die französische Designerin Matali Crasset hat dieses Zuhause in der Pariser Innenstadt entworfen. Die Zimmer der 65 m² großen eingeschossigen Wohnung sind rund um eine zum Wohn- und Essbereich hin vollständig offene Küche angeordnet.

La créatrice française Matali Crasset est l'auteur de ce logement situé en plein cœur de Paris. Le logement s'étend sur un seul étage, sur une surface de 65 m² divisée en plusieurs pièces disposées autour d'une cuisine qui s'ouvre sur une salle à manger et un salon, sans aucune cloison.

De Franse ontwerpster Matali Crasset is verantwoordelijk voor dit huis gelegen in het centrum van Parijs. De woning heeft een verdieping van 65 m² en bestaat uit ruimten die rondom een geheel open keuken zijn georganiseerd.

La designer francese Matali Crasset è l'autrice di questa casa che sorge nel centro di Parigi. La casa è sviluppata su un solo piano di 65 m², e le sue stanze sono ordinate intorno a una cucina aperta sulla sala da pranzo e sul soggiorno, senza tramezzi.

La diseñadora francesa Matali Crasset es la responsable de esta vivienda situada en el centro de París. La vivienda se desarrolla en una sola altura de 65 m², distribuidos en distintas estancias alrededor de una cocina abierta al comedor y a la sala de estar, sin ningún tipo de cerramiento.

DROP HOUSE

Armel Néouze // © Armel Néouze

Entirely fabricated following the standards of industrial prefabrication, the Drop House rests on top of a concrete bed, the only part of the project that was built onsite. It serves as foundation and as a way to connect to the different systems (water, gas, electricity, sewage).

Das vollständig nach den Standards für industrielle Fertighäuser hergestellte Drop House steht auf einem Zementbett (der einzige Teil des Projekts, der direkt auf dem Baugrund gefertigt wurde). Dieses dient als Fundament und als Grundplatte für den Anschluss des Gebäudes an die Versorgungssysteme (Wasser, Gas, Strom, Kanalisation usw.).

Entièrement construite selon les normes de préfabrication industrielle, la Drop House s'appuie sur un fond en ciment (la seule partie du projet construite sur le terrain) qui sert de fondations et de base pour relier le bâtiment aux différents systèmes (eau, gaz, électricité, égouts, etc.).

Het Drop House, dat volledig volgens de industriële prefab normen is vervaardigd, steunt op een cementlaag (het enige deel van het project dat op de bouwgrond zelf werd geïnstalleerd), die fungeert als fundering en basis voor de aansluiting van het gebouw op de verschillende systemen (water, gas, elektriciteit, riolering, enz.).

Interamente edificata secondo gli standard dei prefabbricati industriali, la Drop House poggia su una base in cemento armato, unica parte del progetto costruita sul sito. Tale base funge da fondamenta e serve a collegare i vari impianti (acqua, gas, elettricità, fogna…).

Fabricada íntegramente siguiendo las normas de prefabricación industrial, la Drop House se apoya sobre un lecho de cemento (la única parte del proyecto que se construyó en el propio solar), que sirve de cimientos y de base para conectar el edificio a los distintos sistemas (agua, gas, electricidad, alcantarillado, etc.).

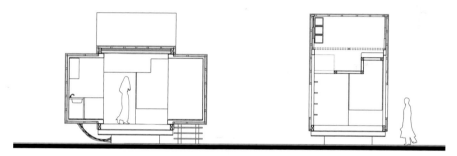

Cross sections

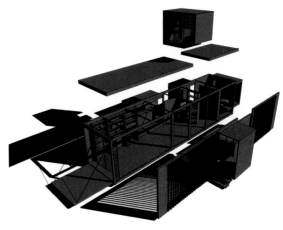

Exploded axonometric plan

Floor plan

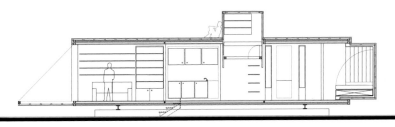

Longitudinal section

222

SMALL

C-2 HOUSE

Curiosity // www.curiosity.jp // © Gwenael Nicolas/Curiosity

C-2 House sits in this mountainous scenery. A wooden walkway crosses through the house and ends at the terrace, where the panorama is spectacular. From the north, the 300-square-foot volume looks like a half-buried mountain home; and from the south, C-2 appears more as a square, two-story, minimalist block.

C-2 House est entourée d'un paysage montagneux. Une passerelle en bois traverse la maison de manière transversale et passe par la terrasse, d'où il est possible de contempler un panorama spectaculaire. Vue du nord, la construction de 84 m² ressemble à une maison de montagne à moitié enterrée, alors que côté sud, elle apparaît comme un bloc minimaliste carré composé de deux étages.

In questo paesaggio montano nasce la C-2 House. Una passerella di legno percorre trasversalmente l'abitazione fino ad affacciarsi sulla terrazza, dove il panorama è spettacolare. Dal lato nord, il volume di 84 m² appare come una casa di montagna per metà interrata; dal lato sud la C-2 si presenta come un blocco quadrato minimalista distribuito su due piani.

In einer bergigen Landschaft erhebt sich das C-2 House. Ein Holzsteg führt quert durch das Gebäude bis zur Terrasse, die einen atemberaubenden Ausblick bietet. Von Norden betrachtet erscheint der Baukörper mit 84 m² Fläche wie eine halb im Boden versunkene Berghütte. Von Süden aus wirkt das C-2 House wie ein minimalistischer Quader mit zwei Etagen.

In dit berglandschap staat het C-2 House. Een houten vlonder loopt dwars door de woning en gaat over in het terras, waar het uitzicht spectaculair is. Vanaf het noorden lijkt het huis van 84 m² op een half onder de grond begraven berghut; vanaf het zuiden doet de C-2 zich voor als een minimalistisch vierkant blok met twee verdiepingen.

En este paisaje montañoso se alza C-2 House. Una pasarela de madera atraviesa la vivienda transversalmente y se asoma a la terraza, donde el panorama es espectacular. Desde el norte, el volumen, de 84 m², parece una casa de montaña medio enterrada; desde el sur, C-2 se muestra como un minimalista bloque cuadrado de dos plantas.

Longitudinal section

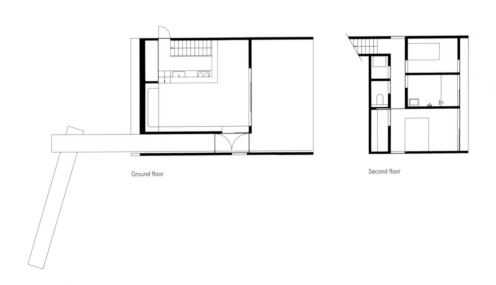

Ground floor

Second floor

OVN HOUSE

OVN Arkitekter // www.onv.dk // © OVN Arkitekter

This house responds to the goal of creating a modern home using only indigenous materials and processes. This brought the designers to focus on quality materials such as Siberian larch, ash wood flooring and natural stone.

Cette maison a été conçue dans le but de construire un logement moderne en utilisant uniquement des matériaux et des techniques autochtones. Afin de respecter cette condition, les créateurs ont opté pour des matériaux de haute qualité, tels que le mélèze sibérien, des sols en bois de frêne et la pierre naturelle.

Questa casa risponde all'obiettivo di creare un'abitazione moderna usando solo materiali e tecniche del posto. Questo ha spinto i progettisti a concentrarsi sulla qualità di elementi come il larice siberiano, i pavimenti in frassino e la pietra naturale.

Bei diesem Haus wurde das Ziel verfolgt, ein modernes Heim ausschließlich unter Verwendung einheimischer Baustoffe und Verfahren zu errichten. Aus diesem Grund entschieden sich die Designer für hochwertige Materialien wie Sibirische Lärche, Bodenbeläge aus Eschenholz und Naturstein.

Dit huis beantwoord aan het doel om met gebruik van enkel autochtone materialen een moderne woning te creëren. Om aan deze eis te voldoen kozen de ontwerpers voor de toepassing van kwaliteitsmaterialen, zoals Siberisch larikshout, essenhouten vloeren en natuursteen.

Esta casa responde al objetivo de crear una vivienda moderna utilizando únicamente materiales y procedimientos autóctonos. Este requisito hizo que los diseñadores se decantaran por el empleo de materiales de calidad, como el alerce siberiano, los suelos de madera de fresno y la piedra natural.

RENOVATION **BY A LAKE**

Wespi & De Meuron Architekten // www.wespidemeuron.ch // © Hannes Henz

This 755-square-foot summerhouse is situated on the outskirts of a small alpine village on the banks of the Swiss-Italian Lake Maggiore. Due to the location on the border, the architects decided to transform the original house, a simple stone building typical of the area, into a section of habitable wall.

Cette maison de vacances de 70 m² est située dans un petit village alpin au bord du lac Maggiore, partagé par la Suisse et l'Italie. En raison de sa situation limitrophe, les architectes ont conçu la transformation de la maison d'origine, un bâtiment simple composé de pierres typiques de la région, ressemblant à une partie de muraille habitable.

Questa casa per le vacanze estive di 70 m² si trova appena fuori da un borgo alpino bagnato dal Lago Maggiore, tra Svizzera e Italia. Considerando la sua posizione, gli architetti hanno progettato la trasformazione della casa originaria, un semplice edificio in pietra tipico della zona, in una porzione di mura del borgo.

Dieses 70 m² große Sommerhaus steht am Rande eines kleinen Alpendorfs am Lago Maggiore, der sich in Italien und der Schweiz erstreckt. Aufgrund der Lage entschieden sich die Architekten für einen Umbau des ursprünglichen einfachen Steinhauses im typischen Stile der Region in einen bewohnbaren Mauerabschnitt.

Dit zomerhuis van 70 m² staat op de grens van een bergdorpje aan het Lago Maggiore, dat deels in Zwitserland en deels in Italië ligt. Gezien de ligging op de grens besloten de architecten het oorsponkelijke huis, een eenvoudig gebouw van typische, uit de streek afkomstige stenen, tot een stuk bewoonbare stadsmuur om te bouwen.

Esta casa de veraneo, de 70 m², está situada en los límites de un pueblecito alpino bañado por el lago Maggiore, que comparten Suiza e Italia. Dada su ubicación limítrofe, los arquitectos plantearon la transformación de la casa original, un sencillo edificio de piedra típico de la zona, en una sección de muralla habitable

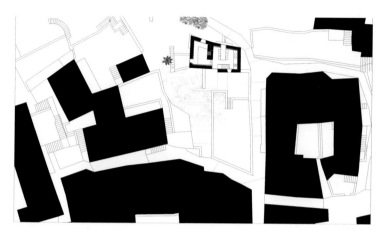

Ground floor plan

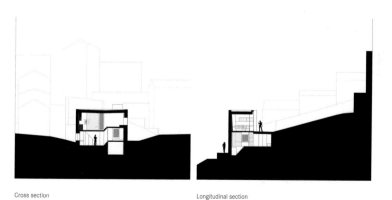

Cross section

Longitudinal section

SOFTBOX APARTMENT

Jakub Szczęsny, Malgorzata Kuciewicz/CENTRALA Designers Task Force // www.centrala.net.pl // © Nicolas Grospierre

Semi-transparent curtains encompass the perimeter of the flat and divide the space in various sections according to the different functions: storage, workplace, media and bedroom. To preserve the open character of the apartment, all the utilitarian functions are centralized in one single block.

Halbtransparente Vorhänge umgeben die gesamte Wohnung und gliedern den Raum in mehrere Bereiche: Aufbewahrung, Arbeitsplatz, Kommunikation und Schlafbereich. Um den offenen Charakter dieses Zuhauses zu bewahren, wurden sämtliche Nutzfunktionen in einem Block untergebracht.

Des rideaux semi-transparents entourent l'appartement et divisent l'espace en plusieurs pièces dotées de différentes fonctions : espace de rangement, lieu de travail, couloirs et chambre. Afin que l'appartement reste ouvert, toutes les fonctions utiles sont concentrées dans un seul bloc.

Halfdoorzichtige gordijnen lopen langs de gehele wand van deze woning en delen de ruimte in diverse zones al naargelang de verschillende functies: opbergen, werkplek, media en slaapkamer. Om het open karakter van het appartement in stand te houden zijn alle nuttige functies in één blok gecentraliseerd.

Tende semitrasparenti lungo il perimetro dell'appartamento suddividono lo spazio in varie zone, in base alle funzioni: ripostiglio, lavoro, tv/tecnologia e letto. Per preservare il carattere aperto dell'appartamento, tutte le funzioni pratiche sono centralizzate in un unico blocco.

Unas cortinas semitransparentes rodean todo el piso y dividen el espacio en varias zonas según las distintas funciones: almacenaje, lugar de trabajo, sala multimedia y dormitorio. Para conservar el carácter abierto del apartamento, todas las funciones útiles están centralizadas en un solo bloque.

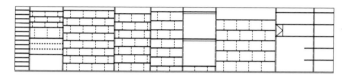

Elevation at built-in cabinet

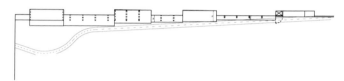

Plan at built-in cabinet

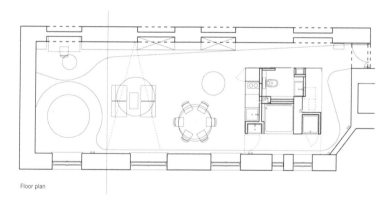

Floor plan

B HOUSE

Atelier A5 // www.a-a5.com // © Sadahiro Shimizu/Atelier A5

B House is situated in a densely populated residential area of Tokyo. A house capable of accommodating two generations of a family had to be built on this 755-square-foot site, providing everyone with their own private space and including a meeting point.

B House se trouve dans une zone résidentielle densément peuplée de Tokyo. Un logement ayant la capacité d'héberger deux générations d'une famille devait s'élever sur ce terrain de 70 m². De plus, il fallait penser à une solution qui puisse optimiser au mieux la surface disponible, en raison de la proximité aux bâtiments voisins.

La B House si trova in una zona residenziale di Tokyo, densamente popolata. Su questo solaio di 70 m² si voleva realizzare un'abitazione che fosse in grado di ospitare due generazioni di una stessa famiglia. Inoltre, data la vicinanza degli altri edifici, era necessario pensare a una soluzione che sfruttasse al massimo la metratura disponibile.

B House steht in einem dicht besiedelten Wohngebiet in Tokio. Auf dem 70 m² großen Grundstück sollte ein Zuhause errichtet werden, das zwei Generationen einer Familie Platz bietet. Aufgrund der Nähe der Nachbarhäuser musste eine Lösung gefunden werden, die die verfügbare Fläche optimal ausnutzt.

B House bevindt zich in een dichtbevolkte woonwijk van Tokio. Op dit stuk bouwgrond van 70 m² moest een woning voor twee generaties van een familie worden gebouwd. Daarnaast diende gezocht te worden naar een oplossing voor de optimale benutting van de beschikbare meters in verband met de nabijheid van de aangrenzende gebouwen.

B House se encuentra en una zona residencial de Tokio densamente poblada. En este solar de 70 m² debía levantarse una vivienda capaz de albergar a dos generaciones de una familia. Además, dada la proximidad de los edificios vecinos, se debía pensar en una solución que aprovechara al máximo los metros disponibles.

REFLECTION OF MINERAL

Yasuhiro Yamashita and Yoichi Tanaka/Atelier Tekuto // www.tekuto.com // © Makoto Yoshida

This small area of just 474 sq. ft. occupies the corner of a lot on which the architects decided to build a polygonal single-family house. The house is comprised of four floors with a total area of 925 sq. ft. The name of the project was inspired by its angular shape.

En raison de sa surface limitée (44 m²) et de son emplacement dans un coin, ce terrain a poussé les architectes à concevoir un logement unifamilial de forme polygonale. De cette manière, une surface de 86 m² répartie sur quatre étages différents a été obtenue. Le nom de ce projet s'inspire de sa forme anguleuse.

La ridotta superficie di questa struttura - appena 44 m² - occupa l'angolo di un terreno che ha spinto gli architetti a progettare un'abitazione unifamiliare a pianta poligonale. In tal modo sono stati realizzati quattro piani ottenendo una superficie totale di 86 m². Il nome del progetto si ispira alla sua forma spigolosa.

Aufgrund der begrenzten Fläche dieses 44 m² großen Grundstücks, das an der Ecke einer Parzelle gelegen ist, entwarfen die Architekten ein vieleckiges vierstöckiges Einfamilienhaus mit einer Gesamtfläche von 86 m². Der Name des Bauprojekts wurde von der winkeligen Form inspiriert.

Het beperkte oppervlak van dit perceel, van slechts 44 m², neemt de hoek van een terrein in beslag, wat de architecten ertoe hebben gezet om een polygonale eengezinswoning te ontwerpen. Zo werden vier verdiepingen gebouwd met een totale oppervlakte van 86 m². De naam van het project is geïnspireerd op de hoekige vorm.

La reducida superficie de este solar, de tan sólo 44 m², ocupa la esquina de un terreno, lo que llevó a los arquitectos a proyectar una vivienda unifamiliar de planta poligonal. De este modo se construyeron cuatro plantas y se obtuvo una superficie total de 86 m². El nombre del proyecto alude a su forma angulosa.

2PARTS HOUSE

Black Kosloff Knott Architects // www.b-k-k.com.au // © Shannon McGrath

This small, wood-covered building is characterized by its use of natural materials. Designed as an addition to bungalow, the structure reflects a double influence that combines Australian style with the architectural qualities of California buildings, exemplified by textured surfaces and the importance of natural light.

Cette petite construction en bois est caractérisée par ses matériaux naturels. Conçue pour être l'annexe d'un bungalow, cette construction reflète une double influence : elle allie un style australien avec des qualités architecturales caractéristiques des bâtiments californiens, telles que les surfaces texturées et l'importance accordée à la lumière naturelle.

Questo piccolo edificio rivestito di legno si caratterizza per l'uso di materiali naturali. Progettata come ampliamento di un bungalow, la struttura riflette una doppia influenza che combina lo stile australiano con le particolarità architettoniche degli edifici californiani, caratterizzati da superfici con texture diverse e dall'importanza della luce naturale.

Dieses kleine, mit Holz verkleidete Haus zeichnet sich durch den Einsatz natürlicher Materialien aus. Die Struktur dieses Anbaus an einen Bungalow wurden von zweierlei Merkmalen beeinflusst: vom australischen Stil (texturierte Oberflächen) und den architektonischen Vorzügen kalifornischer Gebäude (Einfall von viel Tageslicht).

Dit kleine, met hout beklede huis wordt gekenmerkt door het gebruik van natuurlijke materialen. Het is ontworpen als uitbreiding van een bungalow en de draagconstructie weerspiegelt een dubbele invloed die de Australische stijl combineert met de architectonische bijzonderheden van gebouwen uit Californië, die zich onderscheiden door de oppervlakken met texturen en het belang van natuurlijk licht.

Este pequeño edificio forrado de madera se caracteriza por el uso de materiales naturales. Diseñada a modo de ampliación de un bungaló, la estructura refleja una doble influencia que combina el estilo australiano con las peculiaridades arquitectónicas de los edificios californianos, caracterizados por las superficies con texturas y la importancia de la luz natural.

ROOFTECTURE M

Shuhei Endo // www.paramodern.com // © Yoshiharu Matsumara

This studio-residence is created from a single element: continuous metal siding that covers the roof and the walls instead of separating them into different parts. This method (rooftecture), is an attempt to create a continuous residence, a space whose originality stems from the notion of movement that this technique communicates.

Cette maison-studio a été créée à partir d'un seul élément : un parement continu en métal qui couvre tout l'extérieur de la construction, ne séparant pas le toit des murs. Cette méthode (le *rooftecture*) vise à concevoir une construction continue, un espace dont l'originalité découle de l'impression de mouvement produite par cette technique.

Questa casa-studio è composta da un unico elemento: un rivestimento esterno metallico continuo che copre il tetto e le pareti invece di separarle in elementi differenziati. Questo metodo (chiamato *rooftecture*) mira a realizzare un'abitazione «continua», uno spazio la cui originalità parte dalla nozione di movimento che trasmette la tecnica impiegata.

Dieses Wohnhaus mit Atelier basiert auf einem Grundelement: einer Metallverkleidung, die Dach und Außenmauern durchgehenden bedeckt, anstatt diese Bauteile voneinander zu trennen. Diese Bauweise, die „Rooftecture" genannt wird, ist ein Versuch, ein durchgängiges Zuhause zu kreieren, einen Wohnraum, dessen Originalität von der Wirkung der Bewegung herrührt, das dieses Verfahren vermittelt.

Deze studio-woning bestaat uit één element: het dak en de wanden hebben een metalen buitenbekleding waardoor ze in elkaar overlopen in plaats van dat ze van elkaar worden gescheiden. Deze methode, *rooftecture* genaamd, is een poging om een onafgebroken woning te creëren: een originele ruimte waarin dankzij de toegepaste techniek een gevoel van beweging wordt opgeroepen.

Esta residencia-estudio consta de un único elemento: un revestimiento exterior metálico continuo que cubre el tejado y las paredes en lugar de separarlos en partes diferenciadas. Este método (denominado *rooftecture* o techo-tectura) supone un intento de crear una residencia continua, un espacio cuya originalidad parte de la noción de movimiento que transmite la técnica empleada.

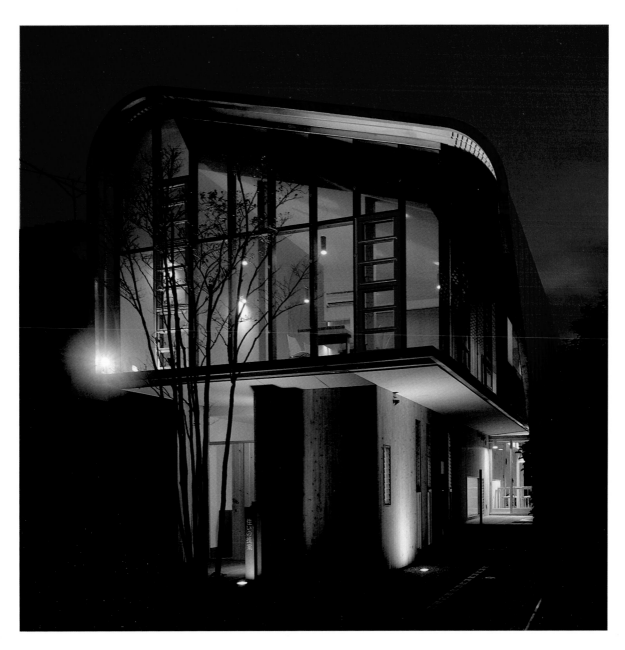

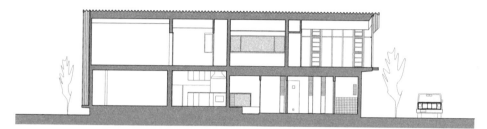

Longitudinal section

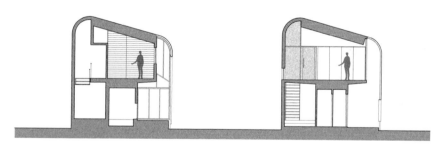

Cross sections

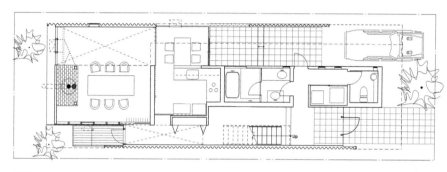

Floor plan

HOUSE **IN BUCHUPUERO**

Álvaro Ramírez and Clarisa Elton // www.ramirez-moletto.cl // © Álvaro Ramírez, Clarisa Elton, Carlos Ferrer

Located in a remote area of the central-southern Chilean coast, this house stands on stilts, which reduce the impact of the building on the ground and allow the water to flow freely. All rooms have panoramic views of the ocean, thus taking advantage of its privileged location.

La maison, située dans une partie isolée de la côte au centre sud du Chili, est soutenue par des piliers sur une pente raide. Ces derniers limitent l'impact de la construction sur le sol tout en permettant à l'eau de courir librement. Toutes les pièces du logement offrent une vue panoramique de l'océan.

La casa, situata in un'estremità remota della costa centro-sud del Cile, poggia su alcuni pilastri in un punto fortemente scosceso. Questa struttura riduce l'impatto del progetto sul terreno oltre a consentire il libero flusso dell'acqua. In tutte le stanze della casa si è cercato di ottenere la vista panoramica sull'oceano.

Dieses Haus steht auf Pfeilern an einem steilen Abhang in einem entfernten Küstengebiet der chilenischen Region Centro-Sur. Dank dieser Pfeiler, die das Wasser ungehindert abfließen lassen, wird die Belastung des Geländes reduziert. In allen Räumen wurde der Panoramablick auf den Ozean betont.

Het huis, dat op een afgelegen punt van de centrale zuidkust van Chili ligt, rust op pilaren die op een steile helling staan. Deze pijlers verminderen het effect van het project op de grond en laat het water vrijelijk stromen. In alle vertrekken van de woning heeft men uitzicht op de oceaan.

La casa, situada en un extremo remoto de la costa centro-sur de Chile, descansa sobre pilares en una pronunciada pendiente. Estos reducen el impacto del proyecto sobre el suelo a la vez que permiten el curso libre de las aguas. En todas las estancias de la vivienda se busca la vista panorámica hacia el océano.

SLIT VILLA

C. Matsuba/tele-design // www.tele-design.jp // © Ryota Atarashi

Small scale is becoming popular in Japan, as illustrated by this house with only 721 square feet located in a densely populated residential area in Tokyo. The kitchen and dining areas are on the ground floor, while the living area is on the second level. The top floor is reserved for the bedroom and a terrace.

Cette maison de 67 m², située dans un quartier résidentiel densément peuplé de Tokyo, illustre la popularité croissante des petits logements au Japon. La cuisine et la salle à manger se trouvent au rez-de-chaussée et la salle de séjour se situe au premier étage. L'étage supérieur est réservé pour la chambre et la terrasse.

Le piccole dimensioni acquistano una popolarità sempre maggiore in Giappone, come dimostra questa casa di soli 67 m² ubicata in una zona residenziale densamente popolata di Tokyo. La cucina e la sala da pranzo si trovano al piano terra, mentre il salotto si sviluppa al piano superiore. Il piano più alto invece ospita la camera e una terrazza.

Kleine Abmessungen werden in Japan immer beliebter. Dies beweist dieses Haus mit gerade einmal 67 m² Fläche, das in einem dicht besiedelten Wohngebiet von Tokio gelegen ist. Küche und Esszimmer liegen im Erdgeschoss, während sich der Wohnbereich in der ersten Etage befindet. Im obersten Stockwerk sind Schlafzimmer und Terrasse untergebracht.

Kleinschaligheid wordt steeds populairder in Japan. Een voorbeeld hiervan is dit huis van slechts 67 m² in een dichtbevolkte woonwijk van Tokio. De keuken en eetkamer nemen de benedenverdieping in beslag, terwijl de salon zich op het tweede niveau bevindt. De bovenverdieping is gereserveerd voor de slaapkamer en een terras.

La escala pequeña gana popularidad en Japón, tal como demuestra esta casa de solo 67 m² ubicada en una zona residencial densamente poblada de Tokio. La cocina y el comedor ocupan la planta baja, mientras que el salón se halla en el segundo nivel. La planta superior se reserva para el dormitorio y una terraza.

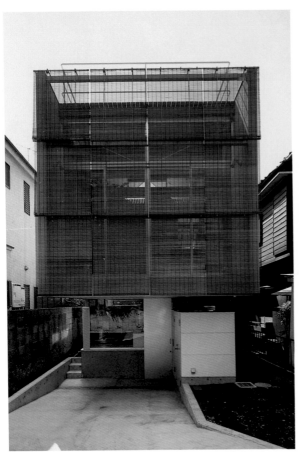

SNOWBOARDERS COTTAGE

Ivan Kroupa // www.ivankroupa.cz // © Martin Rezabek, Libor Jebavy, Ivan Kroupa

This is the classic example of a small structure that is economical and respectful of its environment. The house is used as a retreat by a family during the winter. Because of the poor condition of the original cabin, the architects performed a complete renovation without altering the original dimensions.

Cette construction est l'exemple classique d'une petite structure économique et respectueuse de l'environnement. Elle sert de maison d'hiver pour les propriétaires. En raison du mauvais état de la cabane d'origine, les architectes ont réalisé une rénovation complète tout en gardant les dimensions d'origine.

Ecco il classico esempio di una struttura di piccole dimensioni, economica ed ecocompatibile. Una famiglia utilizza questa abitazione come seconda casa in inverno. Considerando le pessime condizioni della struttura originaria, gli architetti hanno optato per una ristrutturazione integrale, preservando le dimensioni iniziali.

Dies ist das klassische Beispiel für ein kleines, preisgünstiges Gebäude, das äußerst umweltfreundlich gestaltet wurde. Das Haus wird von einer Familie als Rückzugsort für den Winter genutzt. Da die ursprüngliche Hütte in einem äußerst schlechten Zustand war, entschieden sich die Architekten für einen kompletten Umbau, bei dem die vorhandenen Abmessungen beibehalten wurden.

Ziehier een klassiek voorbeeld van een kleine, goedkope en milieuvriendelijke structuur. Dit huis wordt in de winter door een gezin als tweede woning gebruikt. Vanwege de rampzalige toestand van het originele huisje, hebben de architecten voor een volledige verbouwing gekozen zonder de oorspronkelijke afmetingen te veranderen.

He aquí un ejemplo clásico de una estructura pequeña, económica y respetuosa con el medio ambiente. Una familia utiliza esta casa como segunda residencia en invierno. Debido a las nefastas condiciones de la cabaña original, los arquitectos optaron por una renovación integral, sin alterar las dimensiones originales.

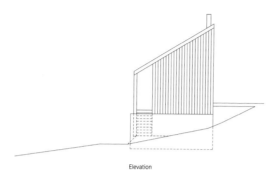

Elevation

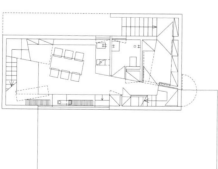

Ground floor

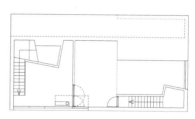

Second floor

CLARABOYA HOUSE

Flemming Skude // flemming.skude@karch.dk // © Flemming Skude

This house was the result of an experiment that was carried out in 1994. The participants expressed their satisfaction after living in it for three months. That structure was very similar to the design used for this project, which is also based on a pyramidal skylight that acted as a focal point to direct light into the interior.

Cette maison est le produit d'une expérience qui a été réalisée en 1994. Les participants qui y ont vécu pendant trois mois ont exprimé leur satisfaction. La structure est semblable au design utilisé pour ce projet : elle se base sur une lucarne en forme de pyramide agissant en tant que point de convergence qui laisse filtrer la lumière naturelle à l'intérieur.

La casa è il risultato di un esperimento realizzato nel 1994. I partecipanti manifestarono la propria soddisfazione dopo avervi abitato per tre mesi. Quella struttura assomigliava molto al progetto utilizzato in questo caso, basato anch'esso su un lucernario piramidale che serve da punto focale per canalizzare la luce all'interno.

Dieses Haus ist das Ergebnis eines 1994 durchgeführten Experiments, bei dem die Teilnehmer drei Monate lang darin wohnten und anschließend erklärten, sie seien äußerst zufrieden gewesen. Die Baustruktur ähnelt dem gesamten Design dieses Projekts, das sich auf ein pyramidenförmiges Oberlicht stützt, welches das Tageslicht direkt in das Innere einfallen lässt.

Dit huis is het resultaat van een experiment dat in 1994 ten uitvoer werd gebracht. De deelnemers gaven hun tevredenheid te kennen, nadat ze het huis drie maanden hadden bewoond. Het genoemde huis leek erg op het ontwerp dat is gebruikt voor dit project, dat is gebaseerd op een piramidaal dakraam dat fungeert als brandpunt om het licht naar binnen toe te kanaliseren.

Esta casa es el resultado de un experimento llevado a término en 1994. Los participantes manifestaron su satisfacción tras habitarla durante tres meses. Aquella estructura se asemejaba mucho al diseño usado para este proyecto, que se basa asimismo en un tragaluz piramidal que sirve como punto focal para canalizar la luz hacia el interior.

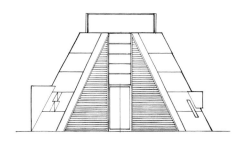

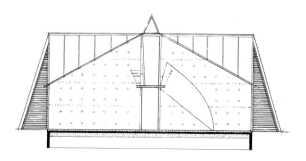

Elevations

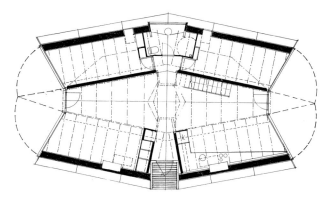

Floor plan

SUMMER HOUSE

Henning Larsens Tegnestue // www.hlt.dk // © Jens Lindhe

This house was designed as a refuge for relaxation and a working place for artists. The project was developed on a 1,076 sq ft surface and had to include a 430 sq ft studio. A single space contains four rooms–studio, foyer, living room, and kitchen–that are connected to a central nucleus by ∫ sliding doors.

Cette maison a été conçue comme un lieu de détente et un espace de travail pour artistes. Le projet a été développé sur une surface de 100 m², comprenant un studio de 40 m². L'espace se divise en quatre pièces (le studio, l'entrée, le salon et la cuisine) qui sont toutes reliées à la structure centrale par le biais de portes coulissantes.

Questa casa è stata progettata come oasi di relax e laboratorio artistico. Il progetto si sviluppa su una superficie di 100 m² con uno studio di 40 m². Un unico spazio abbraccia quattro ambienti (studio, ingresso, salotto e cucina), collegati tramite un nucleo centrale con porte scorrevoli.

Dieses Haus wurde als Rückzugsort für Ruhe und Entspannung und als Arbeitsplatz für Künstler konzipiert. Das Projekt erstreckt sich über fast 100 m² Fläche und sollte ein 40 m² großes Studio enthalten. Ein einziger Raum enthält vier Bereiche (Studio, Diele, Wohnzimmer und Küche), die durch Schiebetüren mit einem zentralen Kern verbunden sind.

Dit huis werd ontworpen als plek om te ontspannen en als kunstenaarsatelier. Het project werd op een oppervlakte van 100 m² uitgevoerd en moest een studio van 40 m² bevatten. Er zijn vier vertrekken (studio, hal, zitkamer en keuken) in één ruimte opgenomen die door een centrale kern van schuifdeuren met elkaar verbonden zijn.

Esta casa se diseñó a modo de refugio para relajarse y taller de artista. El proyecto se ejecutó en una superficie de 100 m² y debía contener un estudio de 40 m². Un único espacio abarca cuatro estancias (estudio, vestíbulo, salón y cocina) conectadas por un núcleo central de puertas correderas.

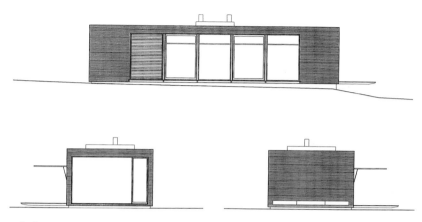

Elevations

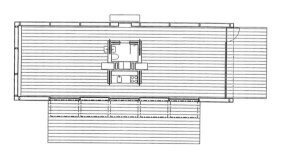

Plan

HOLIDAY HOME **IN THE FOREST**

Besonías Almeida Kruk // www.bakarquitectos.com.ar // © María Masieri/Photo Nider

The project's objectives were to minimize the house's impact on its environment, work within a restricted budget, and minimize the amount of maintenance needed. The house was designed as a first volume—a round glass and concrete prism—and a wooden tower, hidden in the trees, used for all complementary functions.

Le projet a été adapté afin de limiter au maximum l'impact sur le paysage, le budget et l'entretien. La maison se présente comme un premier volume (un prisme rond en verre et en béton) à laquelle s'ajoute une tour en bois cachée entre les arbres destinée à remplir les fonctions complémentaires.

Il progetto mirava a limitare l'impatto sul paesaggio, rispettare un budget limitato e ridurre al massimo gli interventi di manutenzione. La casa è stata pensata come un volume iniziale – un prisma tondo in vetro e cemento – cui si è poi aggiunta una torre in legno nascosta tra gli alberi, destinata alle funzioni complementari.

Dieses Projekt basierte auf den Prämissen, die Belastung der umgebenden Landschaft zu minimieren, sich an das begrenzten Budget anzupassen und den Wartungsaufwand so weit wie möglich zu reduzieren. Das Haus wurde als Baukörper in Form eines Prismas aus Glas und Beton entworfen, der von einem zwischen den Bäumen versteckten Turm aus Holz ergänzt wird, welcher zusätzliche Funktionen erfüllt.

Het project moest een beperkt impact op het landschap hebben, met een laag budget worden verwezenlijkt en zo min mogelijk onderhoud vergen. Het huis werd ontworpen met een eerste deel – een nadrukkelijk prisma van glas en beton – en daarnaast een tussen de bomen verscholen houten toren bestemd voor de aanvullende functies.

El proyecto estuvo condicionado por las premisas de limitar el impacto en el paisaje, ajustarse a un bajo presupuesto y reducir al máximo el mantenimiento. La casa se planteó como un primer volumen –un rotundo prisma de cristal y hormigón– más una torre de madera escondida entre los árboles destinada a albergar las funciones complementarias.

LAKE HOUSE

Bercy Chen Studio // www.bcarc.com // © Joseph Pettyjohn

Due to the simplicity of the lines and materials, Lake House resembles a delicate Japanese garden pavilion, immersed in the rugged Texan countryside. The concrete base, raised above the plot, supports a volume of large windows framed by a steel structure.

La simplicité des lignes et des matériaux de cette construction rappelle un pavillon de jardin japonais entouré d'un paysage texan boisé. La base en béton surélevée supporte de grandes baies vitrées encadrées par une structure en acier.

Per la semplicità delle linee e dei materiali, questo rifugio ricorda un delicato padiglione di un giardino giapponese, immerso nell'aspro paesaggio texano. La base di cemento, sollevata da terra, sostiene un volume con grandi finestroni incorniciati da una struttura d'acciaio.

Durch die einfache Linienführung und die schlichten Materialien erinnert diese Hütte an einen zierlichen Pavillon eines japanischen Gartens, der in die schroffe texanische Landschaft eingebettet ist. Die erhöht errichtete Betonplattform trägt einen Baukörper mit großen Glasflächen, die von einer Stahlstruktur umrahmt werden.

Vanwege de simpele lijnen en materialen lijkt dit huis enigszins op een subtiel Japans tuinpaviljoen dat is op genomen in het abrupte landschap van Texas. De betonnen, boven de grond verheven basis ondersteunt een huis met grote ramen die worden omlijst door een stalen structuur.

Por la simplicidad de las líneas y de los materiales, este refugio guarda cierta semejanza con un delicado pabellón de jardín japonés, inmerso en el abrupto paisaje texano. La base de hormigón, elevada sobre el terreno, sustenta un volumen de grandes ventanales enmarcados por una estructura de acero.

Floor plan

FOLD HOUSE

Mutsue Hayakusa/Cell Space Architects // www.cell-space.com // © Satoshi Asakawa

The concept that lends this project coherence came from experimenting with a system of layers based on old Japanese houses constructed from *fusuma* (sliding doors) and *shoji* (paper panels). This residence explores the architectural potential of using different layers on a structure, as well as the feelings they elicit.

Le concept au cœur de ce projet découle de l'expérimentation d'un système de couches basé sur les anciennes maisons japonaises construites à partir de *fusuma* (des portes coulissantes) et de *shoji* (des panneaux en papier). Cette construction explore la possibilité architecturale d'intégrer plusieurs couches à une même structure, en plus d'analyser les émotions qu'elle suscite.

Il concetto che dà coerenza a questo progetto nasce dalla sperimentazione con un sistema stratificato basato sulle vecchie case giapponesi costruite con *fusuma* (porte scorrevoli) e *shoji* (divisori di carta). L'abitazione esplora le potenzialità architettoniche offerte dall'uso di vari strati all'interno di una struttura esplorando al tempo stesso i sentimenti che suscita.

Das Konzept, das diesem Projekt Kohärenz verleiht, ergab sich durch das Experimentieren mit einem Schicht-System in der Art alter japanischer Häuser, die mit „Fusuma" (Schiebewänden) und „Shoji" (Papierbespannungen) gebaut wurden. Dieses Wohnhaus schöpft das architektonische Potenzial einer Struktur aus verschiedenen Schichten aus und erkundet die Gefühle, die davon hervorgerufen werden.

Het concept dat dit project coherent maakt ontstond uit het experimenteren met een lagensysteem gebaseerd op de oude Japanse huizen die werden gebouwd met *fusuma* (schuifdeuren) en *shoji* (papieren kamerschermen). De woning buit het architectonisch potentieel uit door verschillende lagen in een structuur te gebruiken en onderzoekt tegelijkertijd de gevoelens die zij oproepen.

El concepto que imprime coherencia a este proyecto surgió de la experimentación con un sistema de capas basado en las antiguas casas japonesas construidas con *fusuma* (puertas correderas) y *shoji* (biombos de papel). La residencia explora el potencial arquitectónico de usar distintas capas en una estructura, al tiempo que indaga en los sentimientos que suscitan.

MODERN CABANA

Casper Mork-Unless // www.mork-ulnesdesign.com // © Bruce Damonte

The prefabricated homes have been designed for people who are seeking small spaces or need, in a short period of time, an additional space in their homes. They have standard measurements of 33x33 ft, 33x40 ft, 33x53 ft and 33x83 ft have been conceived so that they can be installed quickly and at a low cost.

Ces logements préfabriqués ont été conçus pour les personnes qui souhaitent disposer de petits espaces ou qui ont besoin d'aménager, en peu de temps, un espace supplémentaire dans leur maison. Leurs dimensions sont standards (10 x 10 m, 10 x 12 m, 10 x 16 m et 10 x 25 m) et ils ont été conçus pour être installés rapidement et à moindres frais.

Queste case prefabbricate sono state progettate per soddisfare le necessità di chi cerca spazi piccoli o desidera disporre in poco tempo di un ambiente aggiuntivo. Hanno misure standard di 10 x 10 m, 10 x 12 m, 10 x 16 m e 10 x 25 m e sono pensate per essere installate in modo rapido ed economico.

Diese Fertighäuser wurden für Menschen entworfen, die sich ein kleines Zuhause wünschen oder innerhalb kurzer Zeit über zusätzlichen Raum an ihrem Haus verfügen wollen. Die Module in den Standardmaßen 10 x 10, 10 x 12, 10 x 16 und 10 x 25 m können schnell und besonders kostengünstig aufgebaut werden.

Deze prefab woningen zijn ontworpen voor mensen die op zoek zijn naar kleine ruimten of die in weinig tijd een extra ruimte voor hun huis nodig hebben. Ze zijn verkrijgbaar in de standaardmaten 10 x 10 m, 10 x 12 m, 10 x 16 m y 10 x 25 m en zijn ontworpen om snel en tegen lage kosten te worden geïnstalleerd.

Estas viviendas prefabricadas han sido diseñadas para satisfacer a personas que buscan espacios pequeños o necesitan disponer, en poco tiempo, de un espacio adicional para sus casas. Presentan unas medidas estándar de 10 x 10 m, 10 x 12 m, 10 x 16 m y 10 x 25 m, y han sido concebidas para ser instaladas de forma rápida y con un coste muy bajo.

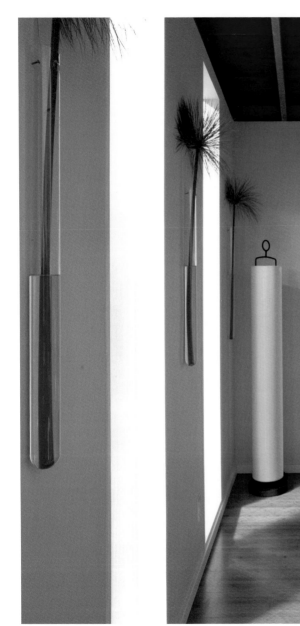

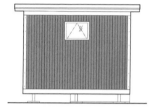
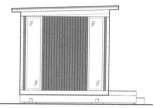

Elevations

Floor plan

Section

TAVOLA

Milligram Studio // www.milligram.ne.jp // © Takeshi Taira

This house, located in one of the busiest parts of Japan's Saitama city, was a challenge for the architects. They set the entire house in the middle of the street, propping the building a few meters above the ground. To do this they placed strong posts to hold up the metal base on which the house was constructed.

Cette maison, située dans l'un des quartiers les plus animés de Saitama City au Japon, a représenté un défi pour les architectes. Ils ont édifié la maison au milieu de la rue, en élevant la construction à quelques mètres du sol. Pour cela, ils ont installé des poteaux solides pour soutenir la base en métal de la construction.

La casa, ubicata in uno dei quartieri più frenetici della città giapponese di Saitama, ha rappresentato una vera sfida per gli architetti. La casa è stata montata interamente in mezzo alla strada e poi puntellata e fissata a vari metri da terra. A tal fine sono stati sistemati grossi pilastri su cui è stata appoggiata la base metallica durante la costruzione.

Dieses Haus, das in einem der belebtesten Viertel der japanischen Stadt Saitama steht, stellte eine große Herausforderung für die Architekten dar. Mithilfe dicker Pfeiler, die die Metallplattform halten, platzierten sie das Gebäude einige Meter über dem Boden mitten an die Straße.

Deze woning, die zich in een van de drukste wijken van de Japanse stad Saitama bevindt, was een hele uitdaging voor de architecten. Zij bouwden het huis geheel midden op straat en stutten het enkele meters boven de grond. Daarvoor werden sterke palen aangebracht waarop de metalen basis tijdens de bouw van het huis steunde.

La casa, emplazada en uno de los barrios más ajetreados de la ciudad japonesa de Saitama, supuso todo un desafío para los arquitectos. Montaron la casa íntegramente en medio de la calle y apuntalaron el edificio unos cuantos metros por encima del suelo. Para ello colocaron fuertes postes en los que apoyaron la base metálica mientras se construía la casa.

Main structure

Second floor structure (hanging)

Third floor structure (put on!)

Complete structure

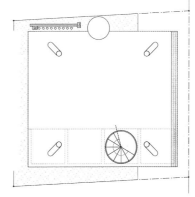

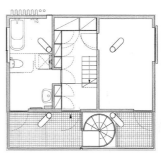

Floor plans

LAKE HOUSE

Casey Brown Architecture // www.caseybrown.com.au // © Rob Brown

This house, erected on a platform to avoid floods, consists of seven pavilions organized according to use. This configuration is determined by the location next to the lake, the climate and the need to regulate temperature. The pavilions collect and store water, and the generated garbage is recycled.

Cette maison, érigée sur une plateforme afin d'éviter les inondations, est composée de sept pavillons organisés selon leurs fonctions. Cette configuration s'explique par l'emplacement de la maison au bord d'un lac, le climat et le besoin d'adapter les températures. Les pavillons récupèrent et stockent l'eau. Les ordures générées sont recyclées.

Questa casa, realizzata sopra una piattaforma per evitare le inondazioni, è costituita da sette padiglioni organizzati in base agli usi che vengono fatti dell'abitazione. La sua configurazione è determinata dalla posizione accanto al lago, dal clima e dalla necessitá di regolare la temperatura. I padiglioni dispongono di sistemi per la raccolta e la conservazione dell'acqua; la spazzatura prodotta viene riciclata.

Dieses Zuhause, das auf einer Plattform erbaut wurde, um Überschwemmungen zu vermeiden, umfasst sieben Pavillons, die je nach Nutzung der Räumlichkeiten angeordnet werden. Diese Struktur ergibt sich infolge des Standorts an einem See, des Klimas und der Notwendigkeit, die Temperatur im Inneren zu regulieren. Die Pavillons fangen Regenwasser auf und speichern es, der erzeugte Müll wird recycelt.

Dit huis, dat ter voorkoming van overstromingen op een platform is opgericht, bestaat uit zeven paviljoens ingedeeld al naargelang de toepassingen van de woning. Deze opbouw is bepaald door de ligging naast het meer, het klimaat en de behoefte om de temperatuur te regelen. De paviljoens verzamelen water en slaan dit op. Daarnaast wordt het voortgebrachte afval gerecycled.

Esta casa, levantada sobre una plataforma para evitar inundaciones, está formada por siete pabellones organizados según los usos de la vivienda. Esta configuración viene determinada por la ubicación junto al lago, el clima y la necesidad de regular las temperaturas. Los pabellones recogen y almacenan el agua, y la basura generada se recicla.

ALUMINUM-RING HOUSE 1

Yasuhiro Yamashita/Atelier Tekuto // www.tekuto.com // © Toshihiro Sobajima

This house has been built from a structure formed by aluminium rings assembled that are used as the base of the structure and as a radiator. In this way, the temperature of the house is controlled by the circulation of cold and hot water through tubes positioned within the rings.

Cette maison a été construite à partir d'une structure formée d'anneaux en aluminium assemblés qui servent de base à la structure et de radiateur. Ainsi, la climatisation du logement est assurée par la circulation de l'eau (froide ou chaude) dans les tuyaux fins situés à l'intérieur des anneaux.

Questa casa è stata realizzata partendo da una struttura composta da anelli di alluminio assemblati che costituiscono la base della struttura e fungono da radiatore. Il condizionamento della casa avviene tramite il passaggio di acqua - fredda o calda - attraverso sottili tubi ubicati all'interno degli anelli.

Dieses Haus basiert auf einer Struktur aus miteinander verbundenen Aluminiumringen, die als Stützelement und zur Klimatisierung dienen. Die Innentemperatur wird mithilfe von Warm- bzw. Kaltwasser reguliert, das durch schmale Rohre im Inneren der Ringe fließt.

Voor de bouw van dit huis is uitgegaan van een draagconstructie gevormd door in elkaar gezette aluminium ringen die als basis van de structuur en als radiator fungeren. Zo wordt de klimatologische aanpassing van de woning uitgevoerd door middel van de circulatie van het koude of warme water door dunne buizen die zich in de ringen bevinden.

Esta casa se ha construido a partir de una estructura formada por anillos de aluminio ensamblados que actúan como base de la estructura y como radiador. Así pues, el acondicionamiento climático de la vivienda se realiza mediante la circulación del agua −fría o caliente− por unas delgadas tuberías situadas dentro de los anillos.

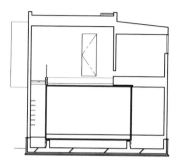

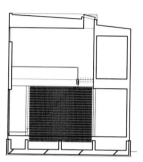

Sections

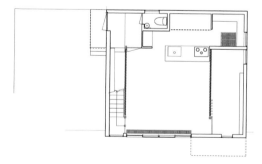

Ground floor

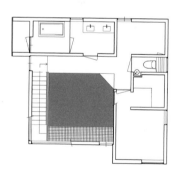

First floor

RICHMOND PLACE

Boyd Cody Architects // www.boydcodyarch.com // © Paul Tierney, Boyd Cody Architects

The intention was to maximize the footprint of the building and extend the living area into the courtyard. The house exploits its section to create a series of interconnected but separate spaces of varying heights and dimensions.

L'objectif de cette construction était d'optimiser la base du bâtiment et d'utiliser les patios pour agrandir la salle de séjour. L'espace de ce logement est optimisé au mieux, divisé en une série de pièces à la fois reliées et indépendantes, de différentes hauteurs et dimensions.

L'intento era quello di massimizzare l'impronta dell'edificio e di ampliare la zona living verso il cortile. La casa sfrutta la sua sezione per creare una serie di spazi separati ma interconnessi, di varie altezze e dimensioni.

Bei diesem Projekt sollte die Grundfläche des Gebäudes maximiert und der Platz des Wohnzimmers in den Höfen vergrößert werden. Durch die optimale Ausnutzung des Querschnitts entstehen mehrere miteinander verbundene, gleichzeitig jedoch unabhängige Bereiche mit unterschiedlicher Höhen und Abmessungen.

De bedoeling van de bouw was de basis van het gebouw te maximaliseren en de ruimte van de zitkamer in de patio's te vergroten. De woning haalt maximaal profijt uit de doorsnede door de creatie van een serie met elkaar verbonden, maar tegelijkertijd onafhankelijke ruimtes van verschillende hoogte en grootte.

La construcción pretendía maximizar la base del edificio y ampliar el espacio de la sala de estar en los patios. La vivienda obtiene el máximo provecho de su sección creando una serie de espacios conectados entre sí pero a la vez independientes de distinta altura y dimensiones.

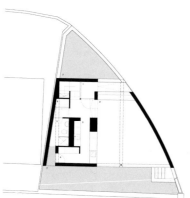

Ground floor

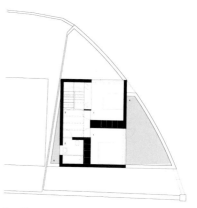

Second floor

PORTO ERCOLE

Fabrizio Miccò // f.micco@awn.it // © Beatrice Pediconi

This small seaside house on the Argentario (Tuscany) is characterized by the sliding panels that divide the various spaces. These sliding panels, made of obscure glass and wooden slats, filter the bright light of the hot season.

Dieses kleine Zuhause in Argentario an der Küste der Toskana zeichnet sich durch die verschiebbaren Paneele aus, die die einzelnen Bereiche voneinander trennen. Diese Paneele aus dunklem Glas und Holzleisten dämmen während der heißen Jahreszeit das helle Sonnenlicht.

Cette petite maison côtière à Argentario en Toscane, se caractérise par des panneaux coulissants qui divisent l'intérieur en différents espaces. Ces panneaux, composés de verre foncé et de lattes en bois, filtrent la forte lumière du jour pendant les mois les plus chauds.

Deze kleine kustwoning in Argentario (Toscane) wordt gekenmerkt door de schuifpanelen die de verschillende ruimten van elkaar scheiden. Deze van donker glas en houten lamellen gemaakte panelen filteren het schitterende licht tijdens de warme zomer.

Questa piccola casa al mare sull'Argentario, in Toscana, è caratterizzata da pannelli scorrevoli che dividono i vari spazi. Questi pannelli scorrevoli in vetro scuro e lamelle di legno filtrano la luce intensa della stagione estiva.

Esta pequeña residencia costera en Argentario (Toscana) se caracteriza por los paneles correderos que dividen los distintos espacios. Estos paneles, construidos con cristal oscuro y lamas de madera, filtran la brillante luz durante la estación cálida.

388

COMPACT

SANDOU HOUSE

Takaharu & Yui Tezuka/Tezuka Architects, Masahiro Ikeda/Masahiro Ikeda Co. // www.tezuka-arch.com // © Katsuhisa Kida

This little house is located just 16 ft from the Seto Inland Sea in the south of Japan. A large front gate protects the house from typhoons and, when open, establishes a link between the interior and exterior. The terraced floor ensures that most of the rooms have views.

Ce petit logement est situé à seulement 5 mètres de la Mer Intérieure de Seto, au sud du Japon. La grande porte d'entrée protège la maison des éventuels typhons et, une fois ouverte, elle relie l'intérieur à l'environnement extérieur. Les différents étages permettent aux habitants de profiter des vues de la mer depuis la plupart des pièces.

Questa piccola abitazione si trova a soli 5 m dal Mare Interno di Seto, nel sud del Giappone. La grande porta frontale protegge la casa da possibili tifoni e, una volta aperta, crea un collegamento tra interno ed esterno. La pianta a gradoni consente di godere del panorama dalla maggior parte delle stanze.

Dieses kleine Zuhause steht gerade einmal 5 m von der Seto-Inlandsee im Süden Japans entfernt. Das riesige Tor schützt das Haus vor möglichen Taifunen und stellt in geöffnetem Zustand eine Verbindung zwischen Innen und Außen her. Dank der abgestuften Form hat man auf den meisten Räumen einen herrlichen Ausblick.

Deze kleine woning ligt op slechts 5 km van de Binnenzee van Seto, in het zuiden van Japan. De grote voordeur beschermt het huis tegen mogelijke tyfoons en als deze deur wordt geopend vormt zij een verbinding tussen het interieur en de omgeving. De trapsgewijze opbouw maakt dat men vanuit de meeste vertrekken uitzicht heeft.

Esta pequeña vivienda está situada a tan solo 5 m del Mar Interior de Seto, al sur de Japón. La gran puerta frontal protege la casa de posibles tifones y, una vez abierta, establece una conexión entre el interior y el entorno. La planta escalonada permite gozar de las vistas desde la mayoría de las estancias.

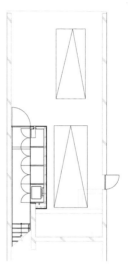

Second floor

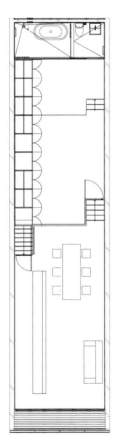

Ground floor

STRAW HOUSE

Felix Jerusalem // www.strohhaus.net // © Georg Aerni

This home has been built with solid panels, prefabricated blocks made up of a layer of very condensed straw, small pieces of wood and a cement core that can be seen in the interior surfaces. Due to its nature and low cost, straw is an excellent material for sustainable construction.

Dieses Zuhause wurde aus soliden Paneelen und vorgefertigten Blöcken errichtet, die eine stark verdichtete Strohschicht, kleine Holzstückchen und einen Kern aus Zement aufweisen, der an den Innenflächen sichtbar ist. Stroh ist aufgrund seiner Eigenschaften und seiner geringen Kosten ein hervorragendes Material für das nachhaltige Bauen.

Ce logement a été construit à l'aide de panneaux solides, quelques blocs préfabriqués composés d'une chape de paille très condensée, de petits bouts de bois et un cœur en ciment qui peut être observé dans les espaces intérieurs. En raison de sa nature et de son coût peu élevé, la paille est un excellent matériau pour la construction durable.

Deze woning is gebouwd met sterke panelen, prefab blokken bestaand uit een laag van stevig samengeperst stro, kleine stukjes hout en een kern van cement die in de binnenvlakken waar te nemen is. Door de aard en de lage kosten van stro is het een voortreffelijk materiaal voor duurzame bouw.

Questa abitazione è stata costruita con pannelli solidi, blocchi prefabbricati composti da uno strato di paglia densamente compattato, trucioli di legno e un cuore di cemento visibile nelle superfici interne. Per le sue caratteristiche e il costo ridotto, la paglia è un materiale eccellente per l'edilizia sostenibile.

Esta vivienda ha sido construida con sólidos paneles, unos bloques prefabricados compuestos por una capa de paja muy condensada, pequeños trozos de madera y un corazón de cemento que se aprecia en las superficies interiores. Por su naturaleza y bajo coste, la paja es un material excelente para la construcción sostenible.

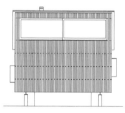

North elevation

West elevation

South elevation

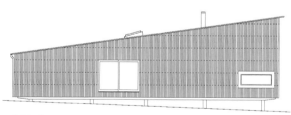

East elevation

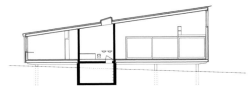

Longitudinal section

Cross section

Second floor

Ground floor

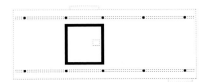

Basement floor

HOUSE **ON THE LAKE**

Michael Meredith, Hilary Sample/MOS // www.mos-office.net // © Florian Holzherr

Its unusual location posed many challenges for the manufacture and construction of the house. The water level changes constantly, varying with the seasons. To overcome this problem, the house was placed on a steel platform supported by pontoons, allowing the water level to fluctuate naturally.

Der außergewöhnliche Standort dieses Hauses brachte viele Schwierigkeiten für die Fertigung und den Bau mit sich, da der Wasserspiegel je nach Jahreszeit großen Schwankungen unterliegt. Um dieses Hindernis zu umgehen, schwimmt das Haus auf einer auf Pontons gelagerten Stahlplattform.

En raison de son emplacement inhabituel, la fabrication et la construction de la maison ont présenté de nombreuses difficultés. Le niveau de l'eau change constamment, car il varie selon les saisons. Ce problème a été solutionné en bâtissant une maison flottante sur une plateforme en acier, soutenue par des pontons qui laissent courir l'eau.

De ongebruikelijke ligging zorgde voor veel problemen bij de vervaardiging en bouw van het huis. Het waterpeil verandert voortdurend al naargelang het jaargetijde. Om dit bezwaar te omzeilen drijft het huis op een stalen platform dat op pontons rust waardoor het waterpeil kan stijgen en dalen.

L'inconsueta posizione della struttura ha causato molte difficoltà nella fase di realizzazione e costruzione della casa. Il livello dell'acqua cambia continuamente in base alle stagioni. Per risolvere questo inconveniente, la casa galleggia su una piattaforma in acciaio che poggia su alcuni pontoni consentendo lo scorrimento dell'acqua.

La inusual ubicación comportó muchas dificultades en la fabricación y la construcción de la casa. El nivel del agua del lago cambia notablemente según las estaciones. Para salvar este inconveniente la casa flota sobre una plataforma de acero que descansa sobre pontones y permite que el agua fluctúe.

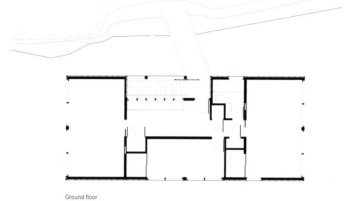

Ground floor

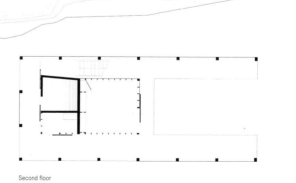

Second floor

4X4 HOUSE

Tadao Ando Architect & Associates // taaa@mx6.nisiq.net // © Mitsuo Matsuoka

This house is a four-story tower, whose square footprint, 13 x 13 ft, gave it its name. The most characteristic element is the top floor, a cube with large windows that projects out from the building, making room for a stairway. This design transforms the architectural space into a refuge for the spirit.

Dieser vierstöckige Turm verdankt seinen Namen der quadratischen, 4 x 4 m großen Grundfläche. Er besticht insbesondere durch die oberste Etage, einen Würfel mit großen Fensterfronten, der aus dem Gebäude hervorragt und somit Platz für eine Treppe schafft. Das Design macht den architektonischen Raum zu einem Zufluchtsort für die Seele.

Cette maison est une tour constituée de quatre étages dont la surface carrée (4 x 4 m) est à l'origine de son nom. L'élément le plus caractéristique est l'étage supérieur, un cube aux larges fenêtres qui fait saillie sur le bâtiment, créant un espace pour installer un escalier. Ce design transforme l'espace architectural en un refuge pour l'esprit.

Deze woning is een toren met vier verdiepingen en een vierkante afdruk van 4 x 4 meter waaraan zij haar naam te danken heeft. Het meest karakteristieke element is de bovenverdieping, een kubus met grote ramen die uit de rest van het gebouw steekt en ruimte voor een trap creëert. Dit ontwerp verandert de architectonische ruimte in een toevluchtsoord voor de ziel.

Questa abitazione è una torre a quattro piani con una pianta quadrata di 4 x 4 m da cui prende il nome. L'elemento più caratteristico è il piano superiore, un cubo con grandi finestre proiettato verso l'esterno dell'edificio, che crea spazio per una scala. Questo progetto trasforma lo spazio architettonico in un rifugio per lo spirito.

Esta vivienda es una torre de cuatro plantas con una huella cuadrada de 4 x 4 metros que le da nombre. El elemento más característico es la planta superior, un cubo con ventanales que se proyecta hacia afuera del edificio y crea espacio para una escalera. Este diseño transforma el espacio arquitectónico en un refugio para el alma.

KURO HOUSE

Hiromasa Mori & Takuya Hosokai / 1980 // 01@takuyahosokai.com // © 1980

The structure of this house is of wood and the exterior walls are also of dark wood. One of the vertexes of the building extends to the front of the lot forming a sharp angle. The house has an area of 1,744 sq ft and was built in a traditional Japanese garden.

Die Struktur dieses Hauses besteht aus Holz, die Außenverkleidung aus dunklem Holz. Insbesondere sticht einer der Scheitel des Grundrisses hervor, der sich in spitzem Winkel zum vorderen Bereich des Grundstücks erstreckt. Das 162 m² große Haus wurde auf einemGrundstück errichtet, das im traditionellen japanischen Stil begrünt ist.

La structure de cette maison est en bois et son revêtement extérieur est en bois sombre. Un des sommets de l'étage attire l'attention car il s'étend vers la partie avant de la construction en formant un angle aigu. Le logement se définit par une surface de 162 m² et il est construit sur un espace vert de style japonais.

De draagconstructie van dit huis is van hout en de buitenbekleding van donker hout. De hoek van het gebouw, die zich uitstrekt naar de voorkant van de kavel, springt in het oog door de scherpe hoek. De woning heeft een oppervlakte van 162 m² en is gebouwd op een terrein met een tuin in traditionele Japanse stijl.

La struttura di questa casa è in legno e il suo rivestimento esterno è nello stesso materiale, ma nella versione scura. Si noti uno dei vertici della pianta che si allunga verso la parte frontale della struttura formando un angolo acuto. La casa si sviluppa su 162 m² di superficie ed è costruita su un terreno con giardino in stile tradizionale giapponese.

La estructura de esta casa es de madera, y su revestimiento exterior es de madera oscura. Llama la atención uno de los vértices de la planta, que se extiende hacia la parte frontal de la parcela formando un ángulo agudo. La vivienda tiene 162 m² de superficie y está construida sobre un terreno ajardinado de estilo tradicional japonés.

0|8

Hiroyuki Arima + Urban Fourth // *yakkko76@rose.ocn.ne.jp* // © Kouji Okamoto

Conceptually, the project made use of contemporary formulas to help define the different uses of the small space. The rooms were divided according to the activities that would take place in them. The architects wanted to explore the potential of the interior and made sure no space followed hierarchical arrangement.

La conception du projet s'est basée sur des formules contemporaines pour conférer plusieurs fonctions à l'espace réduit. Les pièces ont été divisées selon les activités réalisées dans chacune d'entre elles. Les architectes ont souhaité exploiter le potentiel de l'espace intérieur en évitant toute disposition hiérarchique.

In termini concettuali, il progetto applica formule contemporanee per definire i diversi usi di questo spazio ridotto. Le stanze sono state suddivise in base alle attività che vi si dovevano svolgere. Gli architetti hanno voluto esplorare le potenzialità dell'ambiente interno e fare in modo che nessuno spazio acquisisse una posizione gerarchica.

Konzeptuell gesehen wurden bei diesem Projekt zeitgenössische Formeln umgesetzt, die dazu beitragen, die unterschiedlichen Nutzungsarten des begrenzten Raums zu definieren. Die Zimmer wurden gemäß den Aktivitäten aufgeteilt, die in ihnen stattfinden würden. Die Architekten wollten das Potenzial des Inneren des Hauses voll ausschöpfen und sicherstellen, dass die Räume keiner hierarchischen Anordnung folgten.

In conceptueel opzicht maakt dit project gebruik van hedendaagse formules om de verschillende toepassingen van de kleine ruimte te omschrijven. De kamers zijn ingedeeld conform de activiteiten die er moesten worden uitgevoerd. De architecten wilden het potentieel van het interieur optimaal benutten en er zeker van zijn dat bij het indelen van de ruimtes geen enkele hiërarchie zou worden gevolgd.

En términos conceptuales, este proyecto aplica fórmulas contemporáneas para definir los distintos usos del reducido espacio. Las estancias se dividieron de acuerdo con las actividades que debían acoger. Los arquitectos quisieron explorar el potencial del interior y asegurarse de que ningún espacio tuviera una disposición jerárquica.

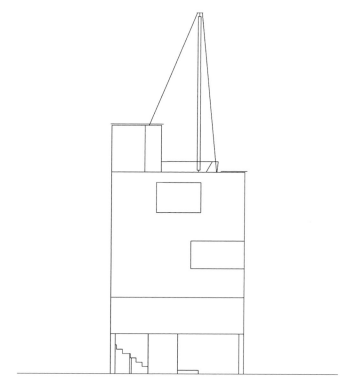

Elevation

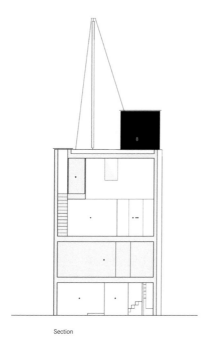

Section

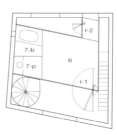

Plan

HAUS **P**

Thaler Thaler Architekten // www.thalerthaler.at // © Hr. Sina Baniahmad

The originality of this small residence becomes evident after a close look at its details. Ingenious ways of making use of the small spaces can be seen throughout the house, like the small centrally located kitchen that is installed in a wood cabinet and can be closed and kept out of sight.

Die Originalität dieses Zuhauses wird nach genauer Betrachtung der Details deutlich. Im gesamten Haus wurden einfallsreiche Strategien zur Raumnutzung umgesetzt, wie z. B. mit der kleinen, zentral platzierten Küche, die in einem Holzschrank untergebracht ist und einfach außer Sichtweite gebracht werden kann.

L'originalité de cette petite construction devient évidente dès lors qu'on en observe les détails. Des techniques astucieuses ont été adoptées pour optimiser l'espace dans toute la maison, telle que la petite cuisine installée au milieu de la construction dans une pièce en bois qui peut être fermée et cachée.

De originaliteit van deze kleine woning springt in het oog nadat de details van dichtbij zijn bekeken. In het hele huis kan men zien hoe de kleine ruimten op vindingrijke wijze zijn gebruikt, zoals deze kleine, centraal gelegen keuken die is ondergebracht in een houten kast, die afgesloten kan worden waardoor de keuken uit het zicht wordt gehouden.

L'originalità di questa piccola abitazione salta agli occhi se ne analizziamo da vicino i dettagli. In tutta la casa emerge un utilizzo ingegnoso dei pochi spazi, come nel caso della cucina centrica incassata in un'armadiatura in legno, che può essere chiusa e nascosta.

La originalidad de esta pequeña residencia salta a la vista tras examinar de cerca los detalles. En toda la casa se aprecian usos ingeniosos de los reducidos espacios, como ocurre en la pequeña y céntrica cocina empotrada en un armario de madera, la cual puede cerrarse y mantenerse fuera de la vista.

RESIDENCE **STEIGEREILAND**

FARO Architecte // www.faro.nl // © Jeroen Musch; John Lewis Marshall

Starting with two premises (spatiality in the design and ecological materials), this house is an experiment that the architect Pieter Weijnen has carried out for himself. The dwelling has three stories and a floating lounge that hangs from the ceiling of the first level. The interior is flooded with natural light and heat through the south-facing glass façade.

Résultat de deux prémisses (un design espacé et des matériaux écologiques), cette maison est une expérience que l'architecte Pieter Weijnen a conçue pour lui-même. Elle comprend trois étages et un *lounge* flottant qui pend du plafond du premier étage. Une grande quantité de lumière et de chaleur pénètrent dans les espaces intérieurs grâce à une façade en verre orientée sud.

Partendo da due premesse (spazialità nel progetto e materiali ecologici), questa casa è un esperimento che l'architetto Pieter Weijnen ha realizzato per uso personale. L'abitazione si sviluppa su tre piani e presenta un lounge galleggiante sospeso al soffitto del primo piano. Attraverso la facciata a vetrate orientata a sud, l'ambiente interno riceve una grande quantità di luce e calore.

Dieses Projekt, bei dem von zwei Prämissen (Geräumigkeit und ökologische Materialien) ausgegangen wurde, ist ein Experiment des Architekten Pieter Weijnen, der damit sein eigenes Zuhause entwarf. Es umfasst drei Etagen und eine Lounge, die von der Decke des ersten Stockwerks hängt. Durch die nach Süden ausgerichtet Glasfassade fällt viel Tageslicht ein und das Haus wird erwärmt.

Dit huis, dat uitgaat van twee onderstellingen (ruimtelijkheid in design en milieuvriendelijke materialen), is een experiment dat de architect Pieter Weijnen voor zichzelf heeft gemaakt. De woning heeft drie verdiepingen en een zwevende lounge die aan het plafond van de eerste verdieping hangt. Door een glazen gevel op het zuiden krijgt het interieur een grote hoeveelheid licht en warmte.

Partiendo de dos premisas (espacialidad en el diseño y materiales ecológicos), esta casa es un experimento que el arquitecto Pieter Weijnen ha realizado para sí. Tiene tres plantas y un salón flotante que cuelga del techo del primer piso. A través de la fachada de cristal orientada hacia el sur el interior recibe gran cantidad de luz y calor.

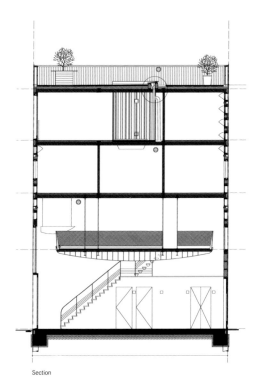

Section

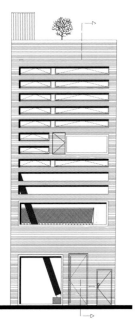

Elevation façade

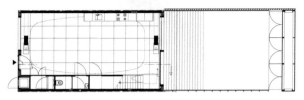

Ground floor

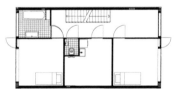

Second floor

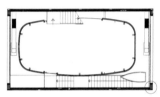

Third floor

Fourth floor

MAISON **FLOTTANTE**

Ronan & Erwan Bouroullec // www.bouroullec.com // © Paul Tahon and Ronan & Erwan Bouroullec

This floating home/studio is moored at Chatou, the island of the Impressionists. An aluminum structure—enclosed in a wooden pergola—denotes the living space which occupies a 16.4 x 75.5 ft. platform. With a total area of 1,184 sq ft, the living and working areas tend to overlap.

Ce logement-studio flottant sur la rivière Sena est amarré à Chatou, l'île des Impressionnistes. Une structure en aluminium, entourée par une pergola en bois, délimite l'espace habitable sur une plateforme de 5 m x 23 m. Les espaces de séjour et de travail sont disposés sur une surface de 110 m² dans des zones qui ne sont pas entièrement définies.

Questa casa-studio galleggiante si trova sulla Senna ed è ancorata vicino a Chatou, l'isola degli impressionisti. Una struttura in alluminio, chiusa da un pergolato di legno, delimita lo spazio abitabile sulla piattaforma di 5 x 23 m. In un totale di 110 m², gli spazi abitabili e di lavoro sono disposti in zone non del tutto definite.

Dieses schwimmende Zuhause wurde in der Seine, ganz in der Nähe des Städtchens Chatou (der so genannten Insel der Impressionisten) vertäut. Eine in eine hölzerne Pergola eingefügte Aluminiumstruktur begrenzt den Wohnraum auf der 5 x 23 m großen Plattform. Auf insgesamt 110 m² wurden Wohn- und Arbeitsbereiche locker miteinander verbunden.

Deze studio-woonboot bevindt zich op de rivier de Seine, aangemeerd naast Chatou, het eiland van de impressionisten. Een aluminium structuur, omsloten door een houten pergola, beschermt de bewoonbare ruimte op het platform van 5 x 23 m, in totaal 110 m². De woon- en werkruimten zijn niet geheel op afgebakende wijze ingedeeld.

Esta vivienda-estudio flotante se encuentra en el río Sena, amarrada junto a Chatou, la isla de los impresionistas. Una estructura de aluminio, encerrada en una pérgola de madera, delimita el espacio habitable sobre la plataforma de 5 x 23 m. En un total de 110 m², los espacios de vivienda y trabajo se disponen en áreas no del todo definidas.

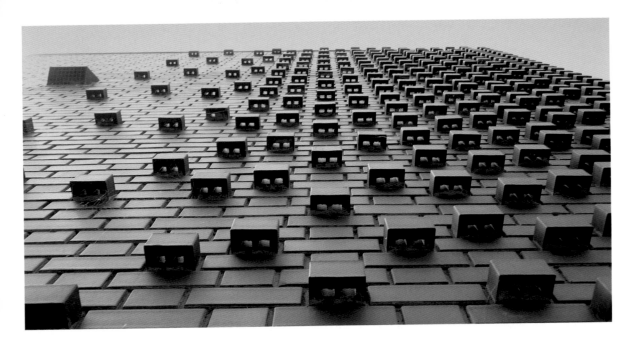

HOUSE **IJBURG**

Marc Koehler Architects // www.marckoehler.nl // © Marcel van der Burg

This 1,506 sq ft home has been designed as a vertical garden. The closed private spaces contrast with the common areas that seem to have been carved into the solid volume. The façade is made up of bricks inspired by the Amsterdam School style of the 1920s. This is a long-lasting and recyclable material.

Cette maison de 140 m² a été conçue comme un jardin vertical. Les espaces privés fermés contrastent avec les espaces communs qui semblent avoir été gravés dans la construction solide. La façade est composée de briques inspirées du style de l'Ecole d'Amsterdam de 1920. C'est un matériau durable et recyclable.

Questa casa di 140 m² è stata progettata come un giardino verticale. Gli spazi privati chiusi contrastano con le zone comuni che sembrano essere intagliate nel solido volume. La facciata è composta da mattoni che ricordano lo stile della scuola di Amsterdam degli anni '20. Si tratta di un materiale riciclabile e fatto per durare nel tempo.

Dieses 140 m² große Haus wurde als vertikaler Garten entworfen. Die abgeschlossenen Privaträume stehen im Gegensatz zu den Gemeinschaftsbereichen, die in den soliden Baukörper gehauen zu sein scheinen. Die Fassade besteht aus besonders langlebigen und recycelbaren Ziegeln im Stile der Amsterdamer Schule von 1920.

Dit huis van 140 m² is ontworpen als verticale tuin. De gesloten privéruimten vormen een contrast met de gemeenschappelijke zones, die lijken te zijn uitgesneden uit het stevige hoofddeel. De gevel is opgebouwd uit bakstenen en is geïnspireerd op de stijl van de Amsterdamse school uit 1920. Dit is een duurzaam en herbruikbaar materiaal.

Esta casa de 140 m² ha sido diseñada como un jardín vertical. Los espacios privados cerrados contrastan con las zonas comunes, que parecen haber sido talladas en el sólido volumen. La fachada, inspirada en el estilo de la Escuela de Ámsterdam de 1920, es de ladrillo, material de larga duración y reciclable.

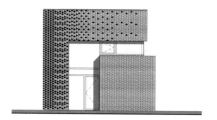

North elevation

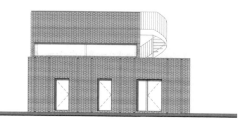

West elevation

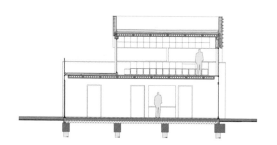

Sections

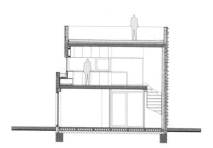

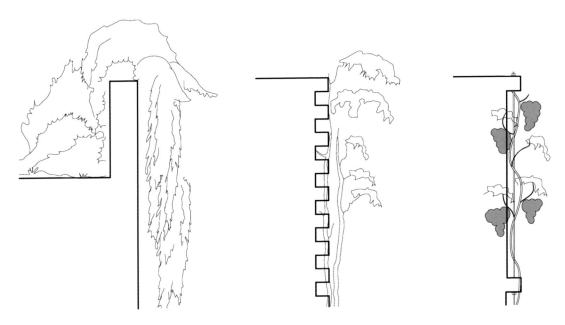

Plants overgrowing façade

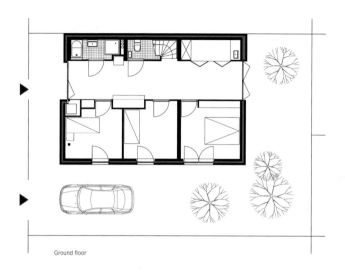

Ground floor

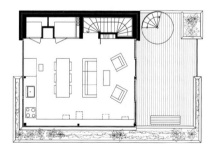

Second floor

THE EYELID HOUSE

Fiona Winzar Architects // www.fionawinzar.com // © Emma Cross

The starting point of this family home is a small, dark terrace. The challenge for the architect was to transform it into a light and airy house with three bedrooms and two bathrooms. In the design, the lid-shaped roof stands out as you have a view of the courtyard and it preserves the intimacy of the interior.

Le point de départ de cette propriété familiale est une petite terrasse sombre. Le défi pour l'architecte a été de la transformer en une maison très lumineuse avec trois chambres et deux salles de bains. La toiture se distingue par le design ; celle-ci est en forme de paupière et offre une vue du patio en préservant l'intimité de l'espace intérieur.

Il punto di partenza di questa abitazione familiare è una terrazza scura e piccola. La sfida per l'architetto consisteva nel trasformarla in una casa molto luminosa con tre camere e due bagni. Nel progetto emerge il rivestimento a palpebra che offre la vista sul cortile salvaguardando la privacy all'interno.

Den Ausgangspunkt für dieses Wohnhaus bildete eine kleine dunkle Terrasse. Die Herausforderung für die Architektin bestand darin, diesen Bau in ein lichtdurchflutetes Zuhause mit drei Zimmern und zwei Bädern zu verwandeln. Das Design besticht durch das lidförmige Dach, das einen Blick auf den Hof bietet und die Privatsphäre im Inneren bewahrt.

Het uitgangspunt van deze gezinswoning is een donker, klein terras. De uitdaging voor de architecte was het om te bouwen tot een licht huis met drie slaapkamers en twee badkamers. In het ontwerp valt het dak in de vorm van een ooglid op dat uitzicht op de patio biedt en de privacy van het interieur beschermt.

El punto de partida de esta vivienda familiar es una terraza oscura y pequeña. El desafío para la arquitecta ha sido transformarla en una casa muy luminosa con tres habitaciones y dos baños. En el diseño destaca la cubierta con forma de párpado que genera una vista hacia el patio y preserva la intimidad en el interior.

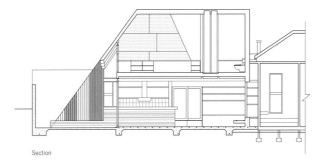

Section

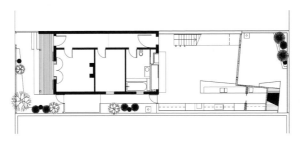

Ground floor

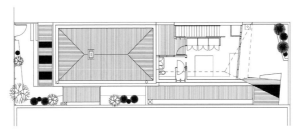

Second floor

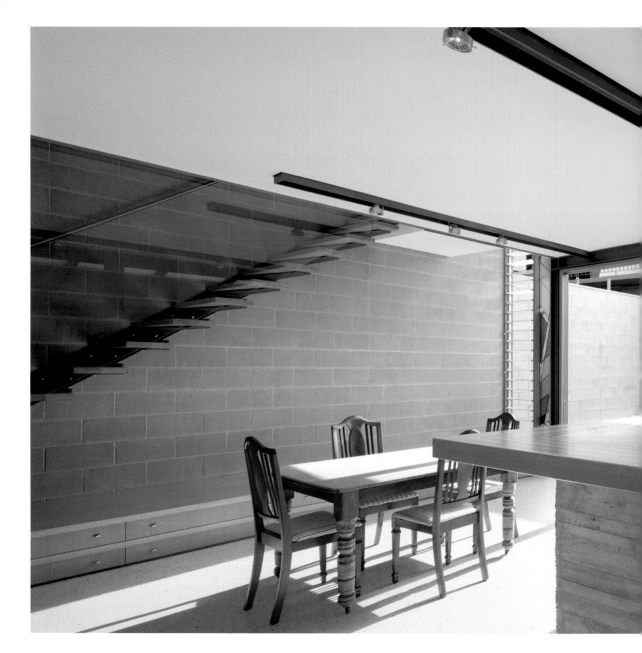

HOUSE **IN MOTOAZABU**

Mutsue Hayakusa, Cell Space Architects // www.cell-space.com // © Satoshi Asakawa, Katsuhisa Kida

This house in Motoazabu consists of three floors of reduced dimensions connected by a spiral stairway. The home has an unusual shape due to the lack of space available for erecting the building. To overcome this inconvenience the architects decided to make use of angles and contrasting elements.

Cette maison à Motoazabu comprend trois étages de petites dimensions reliés par un escalier en colimaçon. La structure inhabituelle de cette maison s'explique par le manque d'espace disponible pour sa construction. Les architectes ont pallié ce manque d'espace en utilisant des angles et des contrastes.

Questa casa ubicata a Motoazabu è composta da tre piani di piccole dimensioni, collegati tramite una scala a chiocciola. L'abitazione si presenta con una forma inconsueta dovuta al poco spazio disponibile per la sua realizzazione. Per superare questo ostacolo, gli architetti hanno deciso di ricorrere ad angoli ed elementi contrastanti.

Dieses Haus in Motoazabu umfasst drei kleine Etagen, die über eine Wendeltreppe miteinander verbunden sind. Aufgrund der begrenzten verfügbaren Fläche für den Bau weist das Zuhause eine ungewöhnliche Form auf. Die Architekten entschieden, die entstandenen Winkel und Ecken auszunutzen und kontrastierende Elemente zu schaffen.

Dit huis in Motoazabu bestaat uit drie kleine verdiepingen die met elkaar worden verbonden door een wenteltrap. De woning heeft een ongebruikelijke vorm vanwege de beperkte beschikbare ruimte. Teneinde dit obstakel uit de weg te ruimen besloten de architecten om contrasterende hoeken en elementen te gebruiken.

Esta casa en Motoazabu consta de tres plantas de dimensiones reducidas conectadas por una escalera de caracol. La vivienda presenta una forma inusitada debido al reducido espacio disponible para erigir el edificio. Con la finalidad de salvar este obstáculo, los arquitectos decidieron usar ángulos y elementos contrastantes.

MODULAR 4

Studio 804 // www.studio804.com // © Studio 804

Speed, quality construction and affordable prices characterize these prefabricated houses. One, two or three bedrooms can be formed simply by moving the closets that serve as partition walls. The only fixed walls in the interior were laid out in parallel lines.

Ces maisons préfabriquées se caractérisent par leur rapidité, la qualité de leur construction et leur prix abordable. Une, deux ou trois chambres peuvent être ajoutées rien qu'en déplaçant quelques armoires qui font office de cloisons. Les seules parois fixes à l'intérieur de la maison sont disposées de manière linéaire et parallèle.

La rapidità, la qualità della costruzione e il prezzo accessibile caratterizzano questo tipo di case prefabbricate in grado di ospitare una, due o tre camere spostando semplicemente gli armadi che fungono da elementi separatori. Le uniche pareti fisse all'interno della casa sono disposte in modo lineare e parallelo.

Die schnelle Montage, die hochwertige Verarbeitung und der günstige Preis zeichnen diese Art von Fertighäusern aus. Lediglich durch Verschieben einiger als Abtrennung dienender Schrankelemente können die Gebäude ein, zwei oder drei Schlafzimmer beherbergen. Die einzigen feststehenden Innenwände wurden gerade und parallel zueinander angeordnet.

De snelheid en kwaliteit van de bouw en de betaalbare prijs kenmerken dit type prefab huizen die een, twee of drie slaapkamers kunnen herbergen door simpelweg een aantal kasten die als scheidingswanden fungeren te verschuiven. De enige vaste wanden binnenin de woning zijn lineair en parallel opgesteld.

La rapidez, la calidad en la construcción y un precio asequible caracterizan este tipo de casas prefabricadas que pueden albergar uno, dos o tres dormitorios simplemente moviendo unos armarios que actúan como separadores. Las únicas paredes fijas del interior de la vivienda están dispuestas de forma lineal y paralela.

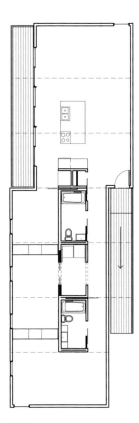

Floor plan